SEX LAW : A LEGAL SOURCEBOOK 0

KF 9325 F75 1990

P9-EAN-908

Sex Law

Sex Law

*A Legal Sourcebook on
Critical Sexual Issues
for the Non-Lawyer*

by
Scott E. Friedman

McFarland & Company, Inc., Publishers
Jefferson, North Carolina, and London

Riverside Community College
Library
4800 Magnolia Avenue
Riverside, California 92506

JUL   '92

To
Lisa Jane
Samantha Kate
Eliza Paige

without your support, this text
would never have been written.
Thank you.

This publication is designed to provide accurate and authoritative information regarding its subject matter. It is sold with the understanding that the publisher and author are not engaged in rendering legal or other professional service. If legal advice or other expert assistance is required, the services of a competent professional person should be sought. (From a declaration of principles jointly adopted by a committee of the American Bar Association and a committee of publishers.)

British Library Cataloguing-in-Publication data are available

Library of Congress Cataloguing-in-Publication Data

Friedman, Scott E.
    Sex law : a legal sourcebook on critical sexual issues for the non-lawyer / Scott E. Friedman.
        p.   cm.
    Includes bibliographical references and index.
    ISBN 0-89950-540-6 (sewn soft. : 50# alk. paper) ∞
    1. Sex and law—United States.   I. Title.
KF9325.F75   1990
346.7301'3—dc20
[347.30613]   90-52665
                                                                CIP

©1990 Scott E. Friedman. All rights reserved

Manufactured in the United States of America

McFarland & Company, Inc., Publishers
  Box 611, Jefferson, North Carolina 28640

Acknowledgments

I would like to acknowledge my gratitude to my father, Dr. Irwin Friedman. Aside from providing me with a wonderful education (along with my mother, Iris Friedman) which, among other things, enabled me to write this book, he provided me with valuable medical resources on several subjects discussed in this book.

I would also like to thank Professor Judy Scales-Trent, professor of law at the State University of New York at Buffalo for her comments on the employment-law sections; Sandra O'Loughlin, Esq., vice-chair of the New York State Bar Association's Committee on Professional Ethics; and Marilyn A. Hochfield, Esq. for their invaluable comments and suggestions on this text. Any errors, of course, are mine.

Thanks to Vincenza Morreale, Patrizia Casali, Betty Stitt and Victoria Kuzenko for their expert secretarial assistance in typing this manuscript.

Last but not least, I would like to acknowledge the support provided by my family—Lisa, Samantha and Eliza. Their encouragement and understanding made this book possible.

Contents

Chapter I

Introduction

This book is intended to be an understandable resource guide, for lawyers and nonlawyers alike, through what has become a complicated maze of laws governing individual sexual rights and responsibilities in the United States. This maze has grown wider and more complex over the past several decades as society grapples with the continuing sexual revolution that poses many novel and often unexpected problems for individuals and society at large. It seems to me that the legal aspects emerging from the sexual revolution are not generally understood, and many of us are often confused about our legal rights and responsibilities concerning sexually related subjects. For example, although it is generally recognized that women may choose to have abortions during the first trimester of pregnancy, the status of laws that may restrict this right — for example, by requiring parental or spousal consent to abortions — is less clearly understood. So too are rights associated with the phenomenon of "surrogate motherhood." Issues such as whether fetuses may be protected from their pregnant mothers' drug and alcohol abuse, whether the law offers herpes and AIDS victims some recourse against their sexual partners who transmitted these diseases by concealing them in the first place, affect many of us, either directly or indirectly.

Individuals with AIDS, from schools and from workplaces, wonder what protection the law offers them as do their classmates and co-workers. Many lesbians and gay males are still confused about their legal rights. These are only some of the many subjects touched upon in this book.

Several thoughts and observations I have about this book are in order. First, this book surveys various federal and state laws on various critical sexual issues in order that you, the reader, may begin to understand your legal rights as well as the rights of others. Leading case precedents throughout the United States are discussed in a manner intended to make sense to readers with no legal background. I have supplied many citations (references) to case or statutory authority, which you may wish to consult for additional information. This book will also help you to frame your questions should you need to consult with an attorney on the subjects discussed below. I believe you will find such discussions much more productive if you have already been "primed" on the law. Because laws vary from state to state, the precedents discussed below, although indicative of a "trend," may not necessarily be followed in your particular state. Accordingly, you should *not* substitute this book for the careful analysis of your attorney, who is familiar with the controlling laws (and their interpretation) in your state or community.

Secondly, merely because an issue or subject is not discussed in this book does not mean it is unimportant or that there are no rights or responsibilities associated with it. It is simply impossible to cover everything in one book, especially when the subject matter is constantly changing and evolving.

Although no book can substitute for a careful analysis of the applicable (current) legal authority by your own attorney, I believe, on the other hand, that you need not be kept in the dark about legal rights and responsibilities on subjects of wide interest. I have written this book because I am unaware of any book like this. Hopefully, this book will help guide your analysis of your rights and responsibilities on "critical sexual issues" and make consultations with your attorney more meaningful.

Chapter II

Rights and Responsibilities Associated with Reproduction

Abortion

Introduction

Prior to the U.S. Supreme Court decision of *Roe v. Wade*[1] in 1973, pregnant women in the United States could generally not legally obtain an abortion unless it was medically necessary. In *Roe,* the Supreme Court held that the "right to privacy" guaranteed by the U.S. Constitution extends to a woman's childbearing decision. This right generally permits a woman to determine (in the first trimester of her pregnancy) whether she wishes to terminate the pregnancy, regardless of the medical necessity.

Roe stirred a great public debate between those advocating a woman's right to have an abortion and those advocating the constitutional protection of the unborn fetus. That debate continues as fervently today as in 1973, and the final chapter on the subject of abortion has surely yet to be written. Indeed, a recent Supreme Court decision, *Webster v. Reproductive Health Services,*[2] received wide public attention because of the general impression that the Supreme Court had the opportunity to reverse *Roe* (and make all abortions illegal) — and it nearly seized that opportunity to do so. Although *Webster* did not overrule *Roe,* the decision is viewed by many as an implicit invitation by the Supreme Court to the states to regulate abortion procedures more strictly. Moreover, the Supreme Court's decision prompted President Bush to press for a constitutional amendment that would ban abortions with few exceptions. Immediately following the *Webster* decision, President Bush went on record as saying that "[the Supreme Court] appears to have begun to

restore to the people the ability to protect the unborn. We continue
to believe that *Roe v. Wade* was incorrectly decided and should be
reversed."[3]

In short, the law on abortion continues to be widely and hotly debated and will surely develop over time. Developments may be expected
to receive wide coverage in the media. The discussion below seeks to
answer some of the more recurrent questions in the area of abortion law.

Roe v. Wade — Guiding Principles of the Abortion Right

> QUESTION: Can pregnant women have an abortion under any
> circumstance or must "good cause" first be established?
> ANSWER: Generally, in the first trimester of pregnancy, a woman
> may choose to have an abortion without having to justify
> her decision.

In *Roe v. Wade,*[4] the Supreme Court established a woman's virtually unfettered right to have an abortion in the first trimester of pregnancy.

In this case, Jane Roe, a single woman from Dallas, Texas, brought
a lawsuit to declare unconstitutional a Texas statute that made it a
crime to have an abortion unless it was necessary to save the life of the
mother.[5]

The Supreme Court held the abortion legislation unconstitutional,
finding that the "right to privacy," guaranteed by the Constitution, is
broad enough to encompass a woman's decision whether to terminate a
pregnancy.[6] The Court based its decision on the possible consequences
to the pregnant woman if refused an abortion, including the mental
and physical distress associated with having to raise an unwanted child,
the problems that could be caused by bringing a child into a family
unable to care for it, and the social stigma that might be attached to
unwed mothers.[7]

The Court emphasized, however, that the pregnant woman cannot
be isolated in her "privacy" in making the abortion decision. In this
regard, the Court determined that it is appropriate for the states, if they
choose, to decide that at some point in time another interest, that of
"preserving and protecting the *health of the pregnant woman*" or that
of "protecting the *potentiality of human life,*" becomes significantly involved.[8] At that point, the woman's privacy is no longer exclusive, and

any right of privacy she possesses must be measured accordingly. The Court then held, in a critical passage that has sparked wide debate, that the State's "important and legitimate interest in potential life ... is at viability," because, the Court explained, "the fetus then presumably has the capability of meaningful life outside the mother's womb."[9]

The Supreme Court then articulated the following principles that have since regulated a pregnant woman's right to an abortion:

1. During the first trimester of pregnancy, the abortion decision is *"left to the medical judgment of the pregnant woman's physician";*
2. After the first trimester of pregnancy, "the State[s], in promoting its interest in the health of the mother, may if it chooses, regulate the abortion procedure [if reasonably related to the pregnant woman's health]";
3. After the fetus becomes viable, the State[s] may, if it chooses, regulate, and even proscribe abortion[s], [unless "necessary for the preservation of the life or health of the pregnant mother"].[10]

Since the Supreme Court's landmark decision in *Roe v. Wade,* state legislatures throughout the United States have been busy testing their authority to impose regulations on a woman's right to abort her pregnancy. In addition, interested third parties — such as husbands and parents — have tested their authority to restrict the exercise of their wives' and daughters' right to have an abortion without their consent. Also hotly debated is the subject of public financial assistance for those women who would otherwise be unable to afford an abortion. The following section discusses some of the rights and responsibilities associated with abortion in the post–*Roe* era.

Regulation of the Abortion Decision

Availability of Federal or State Financial Assistance to Help Pay for the Cost of Abortions

QUESTION: If a woman is unable to afford an abortion, is federal financial assistance available to help her pay for the procedure?

ANSWER: Unless the woman's life is in danger, federal financial assistance is currently unavailable.

In *Harris v. McRae,*[11] the Supreme Court held that the federal Constitution does *not* require the federal government to finance abortions for those who cannot otherwise afford such a procedure—even though the federal governments may, if it chooses, pay the expenses incurred by indigent women that are incident to childbirth.

In *McRae,* the Court considered a constitutional challenge to the "Hyde Amendment,"[12] a federal law (named for Representative Henry Hyde of Illinois, who was instrumental in its passage) that restricts the use of federal funds otherwise available under the Medicaid program to pay for abortions except in very limited instances. The version of the Hyde Amendment considered by the Court in *McRae* provided that no federal funds

> shall be used to perform abortions except where the life of the mother would be endangered if the fetus were carried to term; or except for such medical procedures necessary for the victims of rape or incest when such rape or incest has been reported promptly to a law enforcement agency or public health service.[13]

The Court decided that the Hyde Amendment was constitutional because, among other reasons, it serves to promote the legitimate governmental interest in protecting potential human life.[14] In a passage from the *McRae* decision worth quoting at length, the Court explained:

> ...it simply does not follow that a woman's freedom of choice (recognized by *Roe v. Wade*) carries with it a constitutional entitlement to the financial resources to avail herself to the full range of protected choices ... *although government may not place obstacles in the path of a woman's exercise of her freedom of choice, it need not remove those not of its own creation.* Indigency falls in the latter category. The financial constraints that restrict an indigent woman's ability to enjoy the full range of constitutionally protected freedom of choice are the product not of governmental restrictions or access to abortions, but rather of her indigency.[15]

Since 1981, Medicaid-covered abortions have been allowed only when the mother's life is threatened by the pregnancy. The federal government periodically reconsiders providing federal financial support for abortions under the Medicaid program to indigent women unable to pay for abortions who are victims of rape or incest, as long as these incidents are reported promptly to a law enforcement agency or public health service.[16] To date, such legislation has not been enacted.

QUESTION: If a woman is unable to afford an abortion, is *state* financial assistance available to help pay for the procedure?

ANSWER: Different states offer different types of financial assistance — some very limited and some very broad. Absent state legislation authorizing such financial assistance, there is no "right" to receive aid.

In *Williams v. Zbaraz,*[17] the Supreme Court held that state governments are under no obligation to finance abortions for those who cannot afford the procedure — even though states may, if they choose, pay the expenses incurred by indigent women that are incident to childbirth.

In *Zbaraz,* the Supreme Court used an analysis similar to that which it used in the *McRae* decision to uphold an Illinois law that' prohibited state medical financial assistance for all abortions except those deemed necessary to protect the pregnant mother's life.[18]

One survey reported in 1986 that a number of states then provided public funding only if the woman's life is endangered by carrying the fetus to term. These states include Idaho, Illinois, Indiana, Kentucky, Missouri, Nebraska, North Dakota, Rhode Island, South Dakota, Utah, West Virginia, and Wyoming.[19]

Other states also have provided public funding to pay for abortions where the unwanted pregnancy results from either rape or incest (if promptly reported). These states include Alabama, Arkansas, Delaware, Florida, Iowa, Kansas, Maine, Minnesota, Mississippi, Montana, Nevada, New Hampshire, New Mexico, Oklahoma, Ohio, South Carolina, Tennessee, Texas, Vermont, and Wisconsin.[20] Iowa also provides public financing to help pay for those abortions necessary to prevent the birth of a physically deformed or mentally deficient fetus.[21]

States that have provided public financial assistance to help pay for abortions under almost all circumstances include Alaska, Colorado, Hawaii, Maryland, Michigan, New York, North Carolina, Oregon, and Washington.[22]

At the time of this book's publication, Arizona did not provide any public funding to pay for abortions.[23]

The reader is cautioned that both the continual reassessment by state lawmakers and constitutional challenges to state funding guidelines make the above state-by-state summary subject to change. The reader interested in the current availability of state financial assistance to help

procure an abortion must investigate this matter further with her attorney or other knowledgeable individuals.

> QUESTION: If a woman is unable to afford an abortion in a private
>   medical facility, does the U.S. Constitution guarantee
>   her access to a public facility in which she may have
>   an abortion?
> ANSWER: No.

In *Poelker v. Doe,*[24] the Supreme Court considered the claim of an
indigent woman who unsuccessfully sought to have an abortion in a city-
owned public hospital in St. Louis, Missouri. The abortion which she
sought was *not* a medical necessity. As a result of the hospital's decision,
the woman brought a lawsuit, claiming that the hospital's refusal to provide the desired abortion violated her constitutional rights.[25]

The Supreme Court, in considering the woman's claim, held that
the federal Constitution is not violated by a city "in electing, as a policy
choice, to provide publicly financed hospital services for childbirth
without providing corresponding services for nontherapeutic abortions."[26] The Court explained that "the Constitution does not forbid a
state or city, pursuant to democratic processes, from expressing a
preference for normal childbirth [over abortion] as St. Louis has
done."[27]

This subject was recently reconsidered by the Supreme Court in
Webster v. Reproductive Health Services.[28] This case considered a
Missouri law that, among other things, prohibited the use of public
employees and facilities from performing or assisting in the performance
of abortions not necessary to save the mother's life.[29]

The Supreme Court decided that Missouri's decision to use public
facilities and staff to encourage childbirth over abortion, and its refusal
to allow public employees to perform abortions in public hospitals, was
constitutionally permissible. The Court reasoned that nothing in the
Constitution requires states to enter or remain in the business of performing abortions.[30]

The practical effect of the Supreme Court's decisions is to leave a
pregnant woman seeking an abortion in Missouri (and other states with
similar restrictions) with fewer choices than she may have had before.
Now pregnant women seeking abortions in these states must procure an
abortion in a private clinic, at a doctor's office, or in another state that
permits abortions in public hospitals. Obviously, these alternatives may
not be attractive for many poor women.

Regulation After Viability

QUESTION: As discussed above, under the guidelines spelled out in the Supreme Court's *Roe v. Wade* decision, the states' interest in the fetus becomes meaningful at "the point of viability." What is the practical effect of this standard?

ANSWER: This standard enables states, if they choose, to enact legislation which requires physicians, prior to performing an abortion, to determine whether the fetus is viable. If such tests indicate that the fetus is viable, the states may severely limit the conditions under which an abortion may be performed.

As noted above, the Supreme Court's most recent decision concerning abortion is *Webster v. Reproductive Health Services.*[31] At issue in *Webster* was the constitutionality of a Missouri law, similar to laws in some other states, that, among other things, requires a physician, prior to performing an abortion on any woman believed to be twenty or more weeks pregnant, to ascertain whether the fetus is viable by performing "such medical examinations and tests as are necessary to make a finding of the [unborn child's] gestational age, weight and lung maturity."[32]

In response to a challenge to the constitutionality of this provision, the Supreme Court determined that this requirement was properly concerned with "promoting the state's interest in potential human life...."[33] The Court observed that the Missouri law creates a presumption of viability at twenty weeks of pregnancy. In order to proceed with an abortion at such point in time, a physician must establish by appropriate tests that the fetus is, in fact, not yet viable.[34] The Court observed that "[t]he Missouri testing requirement ... is reasonably designed to ensure that abortions are not performed where the fetus is viable — an end which all concede is legitimate — and that is sufficient to sustain its constitutionality."[35]

The Court then concluded its opinion in *Webster* by noting that because the Missouri law under consideration did not prohibit the performance of all abortions, it would be technically inappropriate to reconsider the underlying abortion right established in *Roe v. Wade.*[36] Whether the Supreme Court will reconsider its position in *Roe v. Wade* when it is technically appropriate to do so remains to be seen.

Regulation of the Abortion
Decision by Spousal Consent

QUESTION: May a woman have an abortion even though her husband objects and wants his wife to have their baby?

ANSWER: The woman may have an abortion without her husband's
consent and over his objection.

Many husbands undoubtedly wonder whether they have the right to prohibit their spouses from aborting "their" child by registering (with their wives or their wives' obstetricians) their opposition to the procedure.

This subject was considered and answered by the Supreme Court in *Planned Parenthood of Missouri v. Danforth.*[37] In this case, a Missouri statute sought to require married women wishing to have an abortion during the first twelve weeks of pregnancy to secure their husbands' consent to the procedure, except in cases of "medical necessity."[38] The Missouri legislature had enacted the law because it believed that "any major change in family status is a decision to be made jointly by the marriage partners"[39] and that "a change in the family structure set in motion by mutual consent [of a married couple] should be terminated only by [the couple's] mutual consent."[40]

The legality of the Missouri law was challenged on the ground that it afforded a husband the right to veto unilaterally a woman's right to have an abortion, even if he was not the "father of the fetus."[41]

The Supreme Court determined that the Missouri law was an unconstitutional abridgement of a married woman's right to have an abortion. The Court explained that "the State cannot delegate to a spouse a veto power which the state itself is absolutely and totally prohibited from exercising during the first trimester of pregnancy.... Since the State cannot regulate or proscribe abortion during the first stage, when the physician and his patient make that decision, the State cannot delegate authority to any particular person, even the spouse, to prevent abortion during that same period."[42]

The Court's reasoning was based, in part, on the reality that if a husband and wife disagree on whether an abortion should be performed, the view of only one, but not the other, could prevail. Because the woman is most directly affected by the pregnancy, the Court believed that the decision should ultimately be hers.[43] Accordingly, the Supreme Court held that a woman's right to have an abortion may not be vetoed by requiring her husband's consent to the procedure.

As interpreted by state courts, a woman's constitutional right to have an abortion, in the face of spousal opposition to the procedure, is very broad. For example, in *Steinhoff v. Steinhoff*,[44] a New York State trial court held that a pregnant woman, concerned about "her appearance, the difficulties of life in this world and family disharmony" was free to have an abortion over her husband's objection even though her husband testified that he was "ready, willing and able to care for the child in the event of a live birth."[45]

Regulation of the Abortion Decision
Through Spousal Notification

QUESTION: May a woman have an abortion without having to notify her husband of her intention to undergo this procedure?

ANSWER: In certain states, a woman may have to notify her husband prior to having an abortion.

Separate and apart from state laws that seek to require a woman to obtain her husband's *consent* before proceeding with an abortion are laws that seek to require a woman to *notify* her husband of her intention to undergo an abortion. Several states currently have "spousal notification" statutes.[46] Although the Supreme Court has not yet ruled on the constitutionality of such statutes, a lower federal court has considered — and upheld — such a statutory spousal notification law.

The case of *Schienberg v. Smith*[47] considered a challenge to a Florida statute that required "a married woman presently living with her spouse to notify her husband of her intent to terminate her pregnancy and to provide him with the opportunity to consult with her concerning the abortion procedure."[48] Florida sought to justify the spousal notification requirement by emphasizing the state's interest in the marital relationship as well as the husband's interest in procreation.[49] A federal appellate court found this justification legitimate and upheld the validity of the Florida statute.[50]

Whether a spousal notification requirement would be upheld in a situation where a pregnant woman seeks to abort a fetus which is the product of an extramarital affair remains to be determined. Opponents to such laws argue that requiring spousal notification in such a situation would unduly burden a woman's constitutionally protected right to abort her fetus.

Parental Control of the Abortion Decision

May the parents of a pregnant minor child regulate their daughter's abortion decision? This question is best addressed in two parts: Can parents veto their minor child's decision to have an abortion? Can a minor child legally choose to have a baby over her parents' direction that she have an abortion?

Regulation of the Abortion
Decision by Requiring Parental Consent

QUESTION: Does a pregnant minor who wishes to have an abortion first need to secure her parents' consent?
ANSWER: Not necessarily.

In *Bellotti v. Baird,*[51] the Supreme Court considered the constitutionality of a state law that sought to regulate a minor child's right to have an abortion by first requiring that she secure parental consent to the procedure. In this case, a Massachusetts law required unmarried pregnant girls under the age of eighteen to obtain the consent of both of her parents before undergoing an abortion.

The Supreme Court first observed that "[a] child, merely on account of his minority is not beyond the protection of the Constitution."[52] It also explained, however, that constitutional principles must be applied with "sensitivity and flexibility" when applied to the special needs of parents and children.[53]

The Court then noted that minor children are often immature and often lack the ability to make informed, reasoned decisions. Accordingly, states may typically — and properly — require minors to notify their parents and/or secure their consent on many "important" subjects, such as, for example, marriage.[54]

The Court distinguished these other kinds of decisions which minors may wish to (or are forced to) make, for which states may properly require parental consent, from the abortion decision. With respect to the abortion decision, the Court observed that potentially severe consequences might follow within weeks following conception — and the decision to proceed with, or abort, the pregnancy cannot be postponed.[55] For this reason, the Supreme Court held that states "*may not impose a blanket provision ... requiring the consent of a parent ... as a condition for abortion of an unmarried minor during the first 12 weeks of her pregnancy.*"[56]

The Court determined that if a state seeks to require a pregnant minor to receive parental consent before securing an abortion, the state must also provide an *alternative procedure* whereby authorization for the abortion *can* be secured without *parental consent*.[57] This procedure would permit the pregnant minor to show either (1) that she is mature enough to make the decision to undergo an abortion independently of her parents or (2) even if she is not able to make the decision independently, the contemplated abortion would be in the minor's best interests.[58]

The Court explained the alternative procedure a state must make available if it chooses to impose a "parental consent" requirement must ensure that a parent is *not* given an absolute veto over the minor's decision to proceed with an abortion. As a practical matter, it must be recognized that the pregnant minor who wishes to exercise this option must secure judicial approval (in lieu of parental approval) of her abortion decision. This requirement opens the door for a judge to restrict a pregnant minor's decision to undergo an abortion by withholding her consent.

Parental Notification

QUESTION: Does a pregnant minor need to notify her parents of her plans to have an abortion?

ANSWER: In certain states, pregnant minors may have to notify their parents.

In *H.L. v. Matheson*,[59] the Supreme Court considered — and upheld — a Utah statute that required a pregnant minor's physician to notify the minor's parents or guardians upon whom an abortion was to be performed. Distinguishing its earlier decision in *Bellotti v. Baird* (which, as discussed above, considered a parental consent statute), the Court found that a parental notification requirement furthered a constitutionally permissible end of encouraging an unmarried minor to seek the help and advice of her parents in deciding whether to terminate her pregnancy.[60] Although the Supreme Court conceded that its decision might inhibit some minors from seeking an abortion, it reasoned that "[t]he Constitution does not compel a state to fine-tune its statutes so as to encourage or facilitate abortions."[61] This decision signaled an obvious retreat by the Supreme Court from protecting a minor's right to privacy.

As this book was being prepared, the Supreme Court decided two important cases addressing parental notification — *Hodgson v. Minnesota* and *Ohio v. Akron Center for Reproductive Health*. These decisions should be consulted for the Court's most recent foray into this area of law.

It was recently reported that

[c]urrently, 31 states have laws requiring parental consent or notification before minors may obtain an abortion. In 11 of those states, including

Minnesota and Ohio, officials are enjoined from enforcing the statutes, while enforcement is allowed in 11 others. The remainder of these 31 states generally do not enforce such restrictions on minors' abortion rights.[63]

The Supreme Court's recent decisions on this subject will surely prompt state legislatures to reconsider their laws.

Right to Give Birth Over Parental Objection

QUESTION: May a pregnant minor choose to have a baby even though her parents would like her to have an abortion?
ANSWER: The few court cases uncovered on this issue have held that the minor has a right to give birth.

Although the majority of contested disputes relating to a minor's abortion decision seem to focus on the requirements of parental consent or notification, the flip side of the coin has also been litigated: May a pregnant minor refuse to have an abortion that her parents insist she have?

This issue was raised in a lawsuit brought in New York State Family Court. In *The Matter of Mary P.,*[64] the mother of a fifteen-year-old girl brought a proceeding to declare the girl a "Person in Need of Supervision" (PINS). The basis of the mother's petition was that her daughter was "pregnant and refused to have an abortion."[65] The mother did not allege that an abortion was medically necessary or even that her daughter lacked the maturity to make an informed judgment about whether to give birth or to have an abortion.[66] The girl simply wanted to give birth.

Relying primarily on the authority of *Roe v. Wade,* the New York court reasoned that "if the right to abort is within the zone of privacy protected by the fourteenth amendment [recognized by *Roe*], the right to give birth exists there as well. It should be beyond question that the decision to give birth is 'fundamental' and 'implicit in the concept of ordered liberty.'"[67] Accordingly, the court rejected the mother's petition and permitted the minor to give birth.

Abortion Counseling

QUESTION: May a woman be compelled by state law to receive detailed information and counseling concerning the physiological consequences of an abortion procedure, against her wishes, prior to undergoing an abortion?

ANSWER: Counseling that becomes a state campaign designed to discourage a woman from procuring an abortion is probably unconstitutional.

In *Thornburgh v. American College of Obstetricians,*[68] the Supreme Court considered a Pennsylvania statute that required, among other things, that a pregnant woman give her "voluntary and informed consent" before having an abortion. The Pennsylvania law sought to ensure that such consent was "informed" by requiring that seven separate pieces of information be delivered to the woman at least twenty-four hours before her consent was given. Five types of information were required to be given by the woman's physician, including (1) the name of the physician who would perform the abortion, (2) the fact that there might be detrimental physical and psychological effects which are not accurately foreseeable, (3) the particular medical risks associated with the particular abortion procedure to be employed, (4) the probable gestational age of the fetus, and (5) the medical risks associated with carrying her child to term. The other two categories of information concerned (6) the fact that medical assistance benefits for prenatal care, childbirth, and neonatal care might be available, and (7) the fact that the father would be liable to assist in the child's support.[69] The Pennsylvania statute also required that the woman who would be undergoing an abortion be shown printed materials that described the fetus and be provided with a list of agencies offering alternatives to abortion. These materials described the "probable anatomical and physiological characteristics of the unborn child in two week gestational increments from fertilization to full term."[70]

In considering a challenge to the Pennsylvania abortion counseling law, the Supreme Court held that the "printed materials required [to be furnished by State law] seem[s] . . . to be nothing less than an outright attempt to wedge the Commonwealth's message discouraging abortion into the privacy of the informed consent dialogue between the woman and her physician."[71] In addition, the Court believed that "forcing the physician or counselor to present the materials and the list to the women makes him or her in effect an agent of the State in treating the woman and places his or her imprimatur upon both the materials and the list."[72] The Court reasoned that such a requirement "comes close to being state medicine imposed upon the woman, not the professional medical guidance she seeks."[73] The Court held such counseling unconstitutional.[74]

The Supreme Court next considered that section of the Pennsylvania law that sought to require physicians to inform pregnant women of "detrimental physical and psychological effects" and of all "particular medical risks" associated with abortions.[75] The Supreme Court determined that this requirement "increased the patient's anxiety and intruded upon the physician's exercise of proper professional judgment," and that "[t]his type of compelled information is the antithesis of informed consent."[76] Accordingly, the Court held this requirement unconstitutional.

The *Thornburgh* decision follows the logic of an earlier Supreme Court decision, *City of Akron v. Akron Center for Reproductive Health,*[77] in which the Supreme Court found an Ohio state law unconstitutional that required physicians to give a detailed description of a fetus, as well as to tell a woman that life begins at conception, prior to performing an abortion.

Right to Recover the Costs of an Abortion from the Father

QUESTION: May a pregnant woman recover the costs and expenses associated with having an abortion perfomed from the putative father?

ANSWER: Maybe.

Case precedent exists that supports the proposition that a pregnant woman may, under certain circumstances, recover the costs and expenses she incurs in undergoing an abortion from the man responsible for her pregnancy. In *Alice D. v. William M.,*[78] a New York court considered the claim of a woman who became pregnant by a man who had advised her not to worry about using birth control because he was sterile. After having an abortion, the woman brought suit to recover her financial damages.

The court found the defendent guilty of negligent misrepresentation, because he "owed a duty to give accurate information to the claimant on the subject of his sterility."[79] The court then held that "[u]nder the facts in this case, it would be incredible and intolerable to state that a woman who becomes pregnant against her wishes and then aborts, has not been harmed, [and] I hold that she has."[80] In order to compensate the plaintiff for her injuries, the court ordered the defendant to pay her "$200 for the cost of the abortion, $4.35 for transportation,

$210 for loss of earnings, and $150 for pain and suffering...."[81] The plaintiff's claim, however, for damages to her "physical condition" was denied.

Whether a woman can recover the costs of an abortion in the absence of such fraud or negligence is less clear. No case considering these circumstances has been uncovered.

Improperly Performed
Abortions that Result in Birth

QUESTION: If a physician negligently performs an abortion, and the pregnant woman delivers a child as a result, can she recover the cost of the failed abortion, the expenses of childbirth, and the costs of raising this child?

ANSWER: Some or all of these expenses may be recovered. (This subject is discussed in the section on wrongful pregnancy below.)

Surrogate Motherhood

Introduction

For would-be parents who are unable or choose not to have their own children because, for example, they are concerned about their age or health risks to the woman, or are concerned about transmitting genetically linked defects to their children, and who prefer not to wait to adopt a baby (which can often take many years) surrogate motherhood offers an alternative. Essentially, a "surrogate mother" is a woman who gives birth for the benefit of someone else.

For surrogate motherhood to work, the following steps must be taken: (1) the interested parents must identify a prospective surrogate; (2) the parties agree that the surrogate will deliver, and the parents accept, the child at birth; (3) the surrogate mother becomes pregnant (typically through either artificial insemination or in vitro fertilization); and, (4) upon birth, the parties must act in accordance with their agreement, and the surrogate mother gives custody and control of the baby to the contracting parents. If a problem develops with one of these steps, the entire process is at risk of collapse. Many of the emerging legal questions concerning surrogate motherhood concern the last step in the above scenario: the parties' failure to act in accordance with their agreement. The legal response to some of these critical questions are discussed below.

The Surrogate Mother's Change of Mind

QUESTION: Can a woman, after agreeing to be a surrogate mother, later change her mind, break her contract with the prospective parents, and keep the baby?

ANSWER: The law in this area is slowly developing on a case-by-case and state-by-state basis. The majority trend appears to recognize that the surrogate mother may be able to keep her baby.

A surrogate's failure to act in accordance with her agreement to turn the baby over to the contracting parents raises the most publicized aspect of surrogate motherhood — the enforceability of the surrogate's contractual agreement.

Majority Trend

The landmark case on the validity of surrogate contracts is *In the Matter of Baby M.*[82] In this case, the surrogate contract provided that the surrogate mother, Mary Beth Whitehead, surrender her baby, known as "Baby M," to William Stern, the biological father, and his wife, in exchange for a fee of $10,000.[83] Baby M had been conceived through artificial insemination, using Mr. Stern's sperm.[84] The Sterns entered into the surrogate contract because Mrs. Stern was infertile.[85] They were anxious to have a child because most of Mr. Stern's family had been killed in the Holocaust and he wanted to continue his bloodline.[86] They chose not to consider adoption because of the potential for delay and concerns about their age and differing religious backgrounds.[87] When Ms. Whitehead changed her mind and decided not to comply with the terms of the contract and keep her daughter, Stern brought an action to enforce their surrogate contract. Their controversy in the courts quickly became headline news across the country.

In this landmark case, the New Jersey Supreme Court ruled that the surrogate contract was void and unenforceable because it violated a New Jersey law prohibiting baby selling or payments in connection with adoptions.[88] The court rejected Stern's claim that the $10,000 was a fee for services rendered, noting that if there was a miscarriage prior to the fourth month of pregnancy, the Sterns would pay nothing even though Ms. Whitehead would have performed the same services.[89] The court also found that the surrogate contract violated New Jersey's public policy of awarding custody on the basis of a child's best interest. In this regard, the court stated that "[t]he evils inherent in baby bartering are loathsome for a myriad of reasons. The child is sold without regard for whether the purchasers will be suitable parents.... The natural mother does not receive the benefit of counseling and guidance to assist her in making a decision that may affect her for a lifetime. In fact, the monetary incentive to sell her child may, depending on her financial circumstances, make her decision less voluntary.... Baby-selling potentially results in the exploitation of all parties involved."[90]

The New Jersey court also emphasized other evils accompanying the surrogate process that were contrary to that state's public policy, stating that the process "guarantees the separation of a child from its mother; it looks to adoption regardless of suitability; it totally ignores the child; it takes the child from the mother regardless of her wishes and her maternal fitness; and it does all this, it accomplishes all of its goals, through the use of money."[91]

Notwithstanding its decision to void the surrogate contract, the New Jersey Supreme Court affirmed the trial court's award of custody to William Stern, the biological father, on the traditional "best interest of the child" standard.[92] The court explained that this decision was based on "strongly persuasive testimony contrasting both the family life of the Whiteheads and the Sterns and the personalities and characters of the individuals."[93]

Minority Trend

A small minority of states have considered and approved the practice of surrogacy. For example, in *Surrogate Parenting Assocs., Inc. v. Commonwealth ex rel Armstrong,*[94] the supreme court of Kentucky, in upholding the practice of surrogacy, distinguished this practice from baby selling because the contract is entered into prior to conception.[95] The court explained the significance of this distinction by noting that the Kentucky law designed to prohibit baby selling[96] is "intended to keep baby brokers from overwhelming an expectant mother or the parents of a child with financial inducements to part with the child."[97] Because the surrogate mother enters into the contract before conception, her decision is *not* based on seeking to avoid the financial consequences of a pregnancy but, on the contrary, "the essential consideration is to assist a person or couple who desperately wants a child but are unable to conceive one in the customary manner...."[98] The court recognized the significance of the contractual provision used by the parties in this case which provided the surrogate mother with a five-day "grace period" in which she could renege on her agreement to relinquish her child to the contracting parties after birth.[99]

Also apparently following the minority trend is New York, in which one of its trial courts held, in a case known as *Matter of Baby Girl L.J.,*[100] that the New York statute that prohibits making certain payments in connection with the adoption of a baby does not foreclose payment to a surrogate mother.

Analysis

Many states have laws that prohibit, as against public policy, the paying of money (or other valuable consideration) for infant adoptions.[101] In the absence of specific legislation on this subject, these laws may control in the event a dispute arises between the parties to a surrogate contract. The surrogate contract may be voided in these states as constituting an improper form of baby selling. Other laws might also be used to affect the outcome of a dispute. For example, statutes prohibiting mothers from receiving compensation for placing a child up for adoption or statutes prohibiting the contractual assignment of a child's custody may also be interpreted to prohibit the practice of surrogate motherhood.

To clarify parties' rights without forcing them into litigation, states are beginning to formulate legislation that address the practice of surrogate motherhood. For example, the practice has now been specifically addressed by the Arkansas legislature, which has statutorily provided, among other things, that a child born to a surrogate mother is the child of the parents *intended* in the contract.[102] Accordingly, the adoptive parents could probably bring an action for specific performance of a contract and compel the surrogate mother to turn over the child in Arkansas.

Proposed legislation in other states range from banning surrogacy completely to regulating the practice, and those seeking to study the practice before regulating it one way or another. A federal statute has even been proposed by Congressman Tom Luken of Ohio that, if passed, would prohibit either advertising for, making, engaging in, or brokering a surrogate contract on a commercial basis.[103] It may be expected that the unanimous decision by the New Jersey Supreme Court in the *Baby M* case, in which a surrogate contract was struck down, will affect the outcome of both proposed legislation and court decisions throughout the United States.[104]

To summarize, the law on the enforceability of surrogate mother-hood contracts is currently in a state of tremendous flux and uncertainty. The reader who requires additional information on this subject is urged to contact an attorney in his or her state.

> QUESTION: Does a biological father whose sperm is used to conceive the child born by the surrogate mother, who is a party to a surrogate contract, have a better chance of enforcing the surrogate contract than a prospective parent who is not the child's biological father?
>
> ANSWER: The likelihood for "enforcing the contract" probably remains the same but the biological father probably has a better chance of being awarded custody of the baby, exclusive of the surrogate contract.

A biological father has an interest in a child wholly separate and apart from that interest which may or may not be created by a surrogate contract. If the father is able to establish his paternity, he may be awarded custody or visitation, depending on the child's best interests. This, essentially, was the result reached by the New Jersey court in *Baby M.*

The reader is advised that some states statutorily prohibit an unmarried sperm donor from establishing his paternity.[105] These statutes may preclude unmarried sperm donors from establishing any interest in their own child under any theory of law. These statutes *may,* however, be unconstitutional (for example, as a violation of the equal protection clause if married sperm donors are statutorily *permitted* to sue to establish their paternity). Readers interested in additional information on this subject should speak to their attorney.

> QUESTION: If the surrogate contract is deemed unenforceable, may a surrogate mother who is awarded child custody receive child support from the child's biological father?
>
> ANSWER: Possibly.

Although no case has been found that addresses this question, it is very possible that a surrogate mother in such circumstances would be able to receive child support and recover her medical expenses from the biological father. Essentially, once a surrogate mother is able to establish paternity, most states require, by statute, that the father pay child support.[106] This principle is discussed in more detail in the section on paternity. It is problematical that anonymous sperm donors, whose privacy is usually maintained, would have such child support duties because the surrogate mother would not know whom to sue to establish paternity.

The Contracting Parent(s)' Change of Mind

QUESTION: What happens if the parents who contract for a baby with a surrogate change their mind and refuse to accept the baby?

ANSWER: This question raises an important gap in the law of surrogate motherhood that needs to be addressed as the use of this practice continues. A surrogate's remedies may well depend on whether the contracting parents include the biological father (i.e., the sperm donor). If this were the case, the biological father may have responsibilities separate and apart from the surrogate contract. If this is not the case, the surrogate mother may be left with only a claim for support against the noncontracting biological father, who probably did not expect to be burdened with child support.

Control of the Surrogate's Conduct During the Pregnancy

Prohibition Against Alcohol and Drug Abuse

QUESTION: May a surrogate be prohibited from using alcohol, tobacco, and drugs during the course of her pregnancy?

ANSWER: Yes, but it may be difficult, if not impossible, to enforce such a prohibition.

It is not uncommon for surrogate contracts to contain provisions designed to promote the healthy development of the fetus by prohibiting the surrogate's use of alcohol, tobacco, and/or drugs during the surrogate's pregnancy.

While such provisions might be "morally enforceable," it is unlikely that they may be legally enforced. Assuming the contracting party can adequately prove the surrogate's breach of such a provision, a court of law can do little, as a practical matter, to prohibit the surrogate's conduct. For example, an order directing the surrogate mother to cease and desist from such conduct would be difficult to secure because courts usually do not enter orders that require the constant monitoring of a party's activity. In addition, compensation for breach of contract that justifies the imposition of money damages typically requires that a complaining party adequately establish the extent of damages suffered as a result of the breach of contract. In this situation, the extent (even the existence) of damages that may result from drug or alcohol abuse would be difficult to prove.

Finally, the contracting party is probably less concerned about collecting money damages for breach of contract by the surrogate than about "collecting" a healthy baby. In short, even if available, legal solutions designed to regulate a surrogate's conduct during the course of pregnancy are probably of little real help to the contracting parents. It may be noted, however, that many courts are beginning to expand a mother's obligations to the fetus during pregnancy. This subject is discussed in the section below on fetal rights. It is possible that future judicial decisions will expand such obligations to surrogate mothers.

Regulation of the Surrogate's Decision to Undergo an Abortion

QUESTION: May a surrogate mother be prohibited by contract from aborting the baby which she has agreed to turn over to the contracting parents?

ANSWER: Probably not.

Should the surrogate mother decide to abort the fetus, there is probably very little, if anything, that the contracting part may do to stop her.

Although it is common for surrogate contracts to include provisions that expressly prohibit the surrogate from aborting the pregnancy in the absence of the contracting parties' consent or medical emergency, such provisions are probably legally unenforceable. As the discussion on the law of abortion above notes, the decision whether to have an abortion is now, with some exceptions, exclusively the woman's. It is unlikely that this protected constitutional right could be "contracted away." Attempts to prevent a surrogate from undergoing an abortion would likely fail on the basis that such a contractual provision is void as against public policy. Contracting parties should realize early on that they may have very little control over this possibility.

Artificial Insemination

Introduction

QUESTION: What is meant by the term "artificial insemination"?
ANSWER: A medical definition of this term is "the introduction of semen into the vagina or cervix by artificial means."[107] The procedure is often used in treating women with infertility problems. Artificial insemination may be performed in one of three separate ways:

1. "AIH": a woman's husband's sperm is used;
2. "AID": a woman uses sperm from a donor (who may be anonymous or known);
3. "AK": a woman uses the combined sperm of her husband and donor.

QUESTION: Is artificial insemination a new process?
ANSWER: No. The first recorded use of artificial insemination in the United States dates back to 1866 when a physician reportedly inseminated six women with their husbands' sperm in a total of fifty-five procedures.[108] Some evidence suggests that artificial insemination was considered as far back as A.D. 220.[109]

Artificial Insemination and the Law of Adultery

QUESTION: Has artificial insemination always been legal?
ANSWER: No. For example, in *Doornbos v. Doornbos*,[110] an Illinois court found a woman guilty of adultery for being artificially inseminated by a donor—even though her husband had consented to the procedure. The child was considered illegitimate. As discussed below, many states have since addressed this issue to ensure the procedure's legality.

State Regulation

QUESTION: Have laws been enacted to address the artificial insemination procedure?
ANSWER: Some states have enacted statutes that address some, but not necessarily all, of the issues arising out of this procedure. Generally, these laws insure that married women who undergo this procedure with their husband's consent are not guilty of adultery.

Many states (from Alabama to Wyoming)[111] have addressed the practice of artificial insemination through legislation.

These laws generally provide that the husband of the artificially inseminated woman is the child's legal father if he consented to the procedure. In addition, these laws typically ensure that the woman undergoing the procedure is not guilty of adultery nor the child illegitimate. It is noted, on the other hand, that a woman who undergoes artificial insemination without her husband's consent might furnish the husband with grounds for divorce, if he is so inclined.

Although these state statutes represent an advance from the days when women could be charged with adultery for undergoing the procedure, many of these statutes concern the practice as applied only to married women, and "ignore the fact that unmarried women also use the AID procedure (as many as 1,500 single women are artificially inseminated annually) and serve only to legitimize the offspring of married women inseminated by sperm other than that of a husband."[112] Only a few states currently have statutes covering insemination of any woman *other than the donor's wife.*[113] Whether and how the laws will develop to address this situation remains to be seen.

QUESTION: Can anyone perform artificial insemination?
ANSWER: Although the majority of states have not addressed this issue, some states and cities including Georgia, Oklahoma, Oregon, and New York City currently have laws that prohibit anyone other than a doctor from performing artificial inseminations.[114] As a practical matter, of course, these laws may be impossible to enforce.

Rights and Responsibilities of Sperm Donors

QUESTION: Does an individual who donates his sperm for use in an artificial insemination procedure, by a single woman, have any rights (and obligations) as a father?
ANSWER: Maybe.

There are very few cases in this area, but those that have been decided suggest that sperm donors *may* be able to successfully assert their rights as a father of the child conceived with their sperm. In *C.M. v. C.C.,*[115] a New Jersey court was asked to consider a donor's claim for visitation rights for a child he helped conceive. In this case, the plaintiff and defendent originally planned to marry but chose to conceive a child by artificial insemination prior to their marriage. Although their physician refused to perform the procedure, the defendant successfully self-inseminated herself using the plaintiff's sperm. The couple later decided not to marry. After their child was born, the plaintiff sought to enforce visitation rights in a legal action — the defendant having objected to voluntarily offering visitation. The New Jersey court, emphasizing that the defendant consented to the use of plaintiff's sperm for conception, in anticipation that he would share in the privileges of fatherhood, awarded the plaintiff visitation rights, reasoning that a child should have "two parents whenever possible."[116]

In *Jhordan C. v. Mary K.,*[117] a California court of appeals considered the case of a man who donated his sperm to an unmarried woman in order that she could be artificially inseminated and raise a child. The sperm donor testified that he agreed to donate his sperm in return for the opportunity to have "ongoing contact with the child, and he would care for the child as much as two or three times per week."[118] The woman testified that she had only agreed to let the donor see how the child looked — but "she did not want a donor who desired ongoing involvement with the child."[119] After a child was born, the donor sought visitation. The mother initially permitted limited visitation but soon thereafter terminated the donor's visitation entirely. Thereafter, the donor filed a lawsuit to establish his paternity.[120]

The court held that, absent a written contract to the contrary (and because such donation was not made to a licensed physician), the sperm donor could be declared the legal father of the child — even though his only relationship to the mother was that of sperm donor.[121]

The court observed that under California statutory law,[122] had a licensed physician been used to facilitate the artificial insemination, the sperm donor, even if a long time acquaintance of the mother, would *not* be considered the legal father.[123]

> QUESTION: Is the likelihood of a successful paternity action affected by the existence of a relationship between the sperm donor and the artificially inseminated woman?
>
> ANSWER: Where the donor becomes known or was known to the recipient at the time of the procedure, the possibility of a successful assertion of a parent-child relationship becomes, as a practical matter, more likely. The paternal ties (and interests) in such a situation would presumably be much stronger than in an anonymous donor situation, as would the temptation to initiate a relationship or maintain an existing tie.[124] Indeed, as a practical matter,

in a situation involving an anonymous donor, it may be impossible to establish paternity because doctors performing artificial insemination in this situation typically do not keep medical records which would identify the sperm donor.[125]

Other Legal Ramifications Springing from Artificial Insemination — A Footnote

Use of the artificial insemination procedure can give rise to a whole host of unforeseen legal questions and problems. These include, for example, questions concerning the rights of a child conceived by artificial insemination to inherit from his legal and/or biological parents, visitation questions which may arise out of a divorce, and questions which may arise from the use of sperm which has been frozen in sperm banks. The answers to these questions continue to develop. The interested reader should seek the advice of an attorney to help resolve particular questions.

Contraception

Introduction

Contraception — the control of fertility — is not a new practice. The ancient Egyptians apparently used a mixture of crocodile dung, honey, and a gumlike substance to prevent conception.[126] The practice, however, was not always entirely legal within the United States. In 1873, the U.S. Congress passed "An Act for the Suppression of Trade in, and Circulation of Obscene Literature and Articles of Immoral Use" (the "Comstock" Law), which provided, in part, that

> [no] article or thing designed or intended for the prevention of conception ... shall be carried in the mail, (and any person who shall mail such articles) ... shall be deemed guilty of a misdemeanor....[127]

After this federal law was enacted, many states passed similar laws that restricted the sale, advertising, or display of contraceptives. Connecticut even went so far as to actually prohibit the use of contraceptives.[128]

After several unsuccessful attempts to challenge the Connecticut law, a group that included the Executive Director of the Connecticut Planned Parenthood, brought the Connecticut law for review before the Supreme Court in a case known as *Griswold v. Connecticut.*[129] In this landmark decision, the Supreme Court held that the Connecticut law violated the right of married persons to practice birth control free from government interference and was, therefore, unconstitutional. The Court explained:

> The present case ... concerns a relationship lying within the zone of privacy created by several fundamental constitutional guarantees. And it concerns a law which in forbidding the use of contraceptives rather than regulating their manufacture or sale, seeks to achieve its goals by means having a maximum destructive impact upon that relationship. Such a law cannot stand in light of the familiar principle, so often applied by this Court, that a "governmental purpose to control or prevent activities constitutionally subject to state regulation may not be achieved by means which sweep unnecessarily broadly and thereby invade the area of protected freedoms." (citation omitted) *Would we allow the police to search the sacred precincts of marital bedrooms for telltale signs of the use of contraceptives? The very idea is repulsive to the notions of privacy surrounding the marriage relationship.*
>
> We deal with a right of privacy older than the Bill of Rights — older than our political parties, older than our school system. Marriage is a coming together for better or for worse, hopefully enduring, and intimate to the degree of being sacred. It is an association that promotes a way of life, not causes; a harmony in living, not political faiths; a bilateral loyalty, not commercial or social projects. Yet it is an association for as noble a purpose as any involved in our prior decisions.[130]

Many legal questions concerning the regulation and use of contraceptives remained after the *Griswold* decision. The discussion that follows considers some of these questions.

Right to Use

Single Adults' Right to Use

QUESTION: *Griswold* established the right of married people to use contraceptives. Can states regulate the right of single adults to use contraceptives?

ANSWER: No.

This question may surprise many readers. It is commonplace that contraceptives are openly sold in drug stores, supermarkets, even vending machines. We all assume single adults use — and have a right to use — contraceptives. This right, however, was not always so clear.

Prior to 1972, the right of single adults to use contraceptives to prevent pregnancy was not firmly established. The Supreme Court assured this right in the case of *Eisenstadt v. Baird.*[131] This case considered a Massachusetts law that provided a maximum five-year term of imprisonment for "whoever ... gives away ... any drug, medicine, instrument, or article whatever for the prevention of conception" except as authorized by state law."[132] As interpreted, the Massachusetts law provided that (1) married persons could obtain contraceptives to prevent pregnancy but only after securing a prescription; (2) single persons could not obtain contraceptives from anyone to prevent pregnancy; and (3) married or single persons could obtain contraceptives from anyone to prevent the spread of disease.[133] The apparent legislative intent of the Massachusetts law was to both deter premarital sex and to regulate distribution of contraceptive articles which were considered by the Massachusetts Legislature to have "undesirable, if not dangerous, physical consequences."[134]

Finding that there was no rational explanation to accord different treatment to married and unmarried persons, the Supreme Court held that the Massachusetts law violated the equal protection clause of the Fourteenth Amendment. The Court observed that "whatever the rights of the individual to access to contraceptives may be, the rights must be the same for the unmarried and the married alike."[135] Relying on its earlier decision in *Griswold v. Connecticut,* the Court explained, in a passage worth quoting at length, that

> It is true that in *Griswold* the right of privacy in question inhered in the marital relationship. Yet the marital couple is not an independent entity with a mind and heart of its own, but an association of two individuals each with the separate intellectual and emotional makeup. If the right of privacy means anything, it is the right of the individual, married or single, to be free from unwarranted governmental intrusion into matters so fundamentally effecting a person as the decision to bear or beget a child.[136]

Since *Eisenstadt,* a single person's right to use contraceptives has been firmly entrenched.

Minors' Right to Use

QUESTION: Do minors have a legal right to use contraceptives?
ANSWER: Yes.

Several years after *Eisenstadt,* the Supreme Court considered the constitutionality of a New York law that, among other things, made it a crime for any person to sell or distribute any contraceptive of any kind to a minor under the age of sixteen. In *Carey v. Population Services International,*[137] the Court heard a challenge brought by distributors of contraceptives who argued that the New York law was an unwarranted and unconstitutional infringement of a fundamental aspect of personal liberty.

The Supreme Court, after acknowledging the right of individuals, married or single, to be free of "unwarranted governmental intrusion into matters so fundamentally effecting a person as the decision whether to bear or beget a child,"[138] observed that this privacy right does not automatically invalidate every state regulation concerning the use of contraceptives. The Court stated that "the business of manufacturing and selling contraceptives may be regulated in ways that do not infringe protected individual choices."[139] The Court stated, however, that a total prohibition against the sale of contraceptives would "intrude upon individual decisions in matters of procreation and contraception as harshly as a direct ban on their use."[140] Only laws which regulate a compelling state interest, and which are carefully drawn to protect only that interest, will be upheld.

With respect to the New York law which prohibited the distribution of contraceptives to individuals under the age of sixteen, the state argued that this provision was designed as a permissible regulation of the morality of minors, in "furtherance of the State's policy against promiscuous sexual intercourse among the young."[141]

The Supreme Court rejected this argument. Noting that states could not impose a parental consent requirement on a minor's decision to abort a pregnancy, the Court reasoned that "the constitutionality of a blanket prohibition of the distribution of contraceptives to minors is, a fortiori, foreclosed."[142] In other words, the Court reasoned that if a pregnant minor could proceed with an abortion, that same minor should surely be permitted to use contraceptives, so as to prevent a pregnancy in the first instance.

Parental Right to Control Minor Child's Use of Contraceptives

Right to Control Supply to Minor

QUESTION: Do parents have a right to be notified that contraceptives have been provided to their minor child?

ANSWER: Such "right" does not yet appear to have been judicially recognized.

There currently does not appear to be any case in which either a physician or other individual (e.g. pharmacist) has been found guilty under any criminal law or liable under civil law for providing either information about contraception or actual contraceptives to a minor.[143]

One of the leading decisions on this subject is *Doe v. Irwin*.[144] In this case, the parents of a sixteen-year-old girl who received contraceptives from a publicly run family planning center brought suit against the center and members of the county health department. The parents, who were not notified of the center's distribution of contraceptives to their child, alleged that the center's action deprived them of their constitutional rights.[145] The Federal Court of Appeals for the Sixth Circuit rejected the parents' claims and held that the center had no constitutional obligation to notify parents before distributing contraceptives to their minor children.[146]

Right to Regulate Sex Education Courses in School

QUESTION: Is it constitutionally permissible to teach sex education courses to minor children in public schools?

ANSWER: This question can only be answered by the reader verifying the law in his or her community. It may be noted, by way of example, that this issue was the subject of a legal action in California. In *Citizens for Parental Rights v. San Mateo County Board of Education*,[147] the constitutionality of providing sex education classes for students as young as ten was upheld. The court explained its decision as follows:

> ...absent some serious contention of harm to the mental or physical health of the children of this state or to the public safety, peace or order or welfare, a mere personal difference of opinion as to the curriculum which is taught in one public school

system does not give rise to a constitutional right in the private citizen to control exposure to knowledge.[148]

It is noted that the California school program permitted parents to withdraw their children upon written request. Whether a similar result would have been reached if class attendance was mandatory is an interesting questions.

Manufacturer's Liability for Supply of Defective Contraceptives

Use of Defective Contraception That Results in Conception

QUESTION: If the use of defectively manufactured contraception results in conception, is the manufacturer liable for damages?

ANSWER: Many states recognize that such a consequence may give rise to a claim for "wrongful pregnancy" and entitle the parents to money damages as compensation for their "damages." These claims are discussed in detail below in the section "Rights of the Unborn."

Manufacturer's Liability for Casually Related Personal Injury

QUESTION: If the use of improperly designed or manufactured contraceptives cause an individual to suffer personal injury, is the manufacturer liable for money damages to compensate the individual for her injuries?

ANSWER: Very possibly.

An injured party's ability to recover money damages against the party causing such injury depends, of course, upon having a proper legal basis for the claim and the evidence offered in support of such claim. Bearing these general parameters in mind, it is well known that many women have been injured by their use of certain types of contraceptives. Perhaps the best known example of a contraceptive causing personal injury is that of the Dalkon Shield. The Dalkon Shield, made of flexible plastic, conformed to the shape of the uterine cavity to prevent its expulsion. When the Shield was removed, the uterus could be cut by its serrated edges. Bacteria would then be drawn from the vagina into the otherwise sterile uterine cavity, causing infection.[149]

From 1970 through 1974 (when distribution of the Dalkon Shield was suspended) approximately 2.2 million Dalkon Shields were inserted in women throughout the United States.[150] Women who were injured by their use of the Dalkon Shields brought lawsuits seeking to recover both compensatory and punitive damages. Suits were brought under a variety of theories, such as strict products liability, breach of warranty, negligence, and fraud. Suits were brought against the Dalkon Shield's manufacturer (A.H. Robins Co.), as well as its local suppliers and individual physicians who recommended and inserted the Shield. Many of these cases resulted in huge awards for the injured women. For example, in one case, an injured woman recovered $600,000 in compensatory damages and $6.2 million in punitive damages.[151] The A.H. Robins Co. was later forced to file for protection under Chapter 11 of the Bankruptcy Code because of the thousands of claims that had been filed against it.

> QUESTION: If a woman's use of contraceptives causes injury to children she later conceives, can her children recover money damages for their injuries?
> ANSWER: Possibly.

Although, as noted below in the section on the wrongful infliction of preconception injuries, courts are very reluctant to allow claims for damages sustained by an individual prior to that individual's conception, there is some case precedent that supports this type of claim. In *Jorgensen v. Meade Johnson Laboratories, Inc.,*[152] a woman took birth control pills which were manufactured by the defendant. Her use of these pills caused her to sustain genetic aberrations in the chromosomal structure of her ovum.[153] As a result of these aberrations, the plaintiff's twins, which she later conceived, suffered from Asiatic Mongolism. The court of appeals recognized the infants' right of recovery, reasoning that if an infant was denied recovery for a preconception injury, then "an infant suffering personal injury from a defective food product, manufactured before his conception, would be without remedy."[154]

This question is discussed at greater length below in the section on the wrongful infliction of preconception injuries.

Failure to Use Contraception Because of Deceptive Lover's False Assurances

QUESTION: If one person assures another that their use of contraception is unnecessary to prevent pregnancy (because, for example, of the assuring person's infertility or use of a nonobvious form of contraception) and, in reliance thereon, the party being assured does not use contraception, is there liability for damages if a pregnancy results?

ANSWER: Possibly.

Although this area of law is continuing to develop (in an attempt to keep pace with the variety of deceptive acts which may result in pregnancy), some courts have already held that deceptive lovers might be liable for damages which result in pregnancy. For example, in *Barbara A. v. John G.,*[155] a California court considered the claim of a plaintiff who had advised the defendant to use a condom prior to intercourse, saying that she would not have intercourse with him if she could get pregnant. The defendant explained to her that he couldn't "possibly get anyone pregnant."[156] The plaintiff understood this statement to mean that he was sterile by nature or as the result of a vasectomy. This was not the case and the plaintiff became pregnant. The pregnancy was "ectopic" and the plaintiff was forced to undergo surgery in which her fallopian tube was removed—rendering her sterile. The plaintiff thereafter brought this lawsuit to seek monetary compensation for the unplanned pregnancy and resulting injury.

The California court held the plaintiff's consent to intercourse was improperly secured (and so vitiated) by the defendant's fraudulent statement as to his sterility. Accordingly, the court found that the defendant's impregnation of the plaintiff was a harmful and offensive contact which amounted to (compensable) battery.[157]

In addition, as noted above, a woman who becomes pregnant after having been lied to may, in some states, be able to recover the costs and expenses of an abortion.

QUESTION: If a woman falsely advises a man that she is using birth control can the man be found liable for child support should she become pregnant?

ANSWER: Yes.

A man in this situation may expect to be found liable for child support even if he is able to raise as a defense that the mother lied by stating that "she was on the pill" but wasn't. The most frequently cited case in this area appears to be *Pamela P. v. Frank S.*[158] In this case, the plaintiff falsely advised the defendant that she was using contraception when, in fact, she secretly wanted to have a baby.[159] After the baby was born, the woman commenced a lawsuit in New York to compel the defendant to pay child support. The defendant argued that to burden him with the (financial) responsibilities of paternity in light of the plaintiff's deceit would be an unconstitutional interference with his right to choose whether or not to procreate. The New York Supreme Court held that the father's defense was irrelevant in a child support proceeding. The court further held that once paternity is established, the only factors to be considered in a child support proceeding are the child's needs and the parent's means.[160] The woman's deceit in this case was found irrelevant.

A Michigan court adopted similar reasoning in a case captioned *Faske v. Bonanno.*[161] This court explained:

> Parents have an obligation to support their children and the circumstances of a child's conception do not give rise to an exception to that rule . . . the child [should not] suffer from one of the parents' fault regarding the conception.[162]

Sterilization

Introduction

Sterilization has become one of the world's most popular methods of exercising birth control. It is reported that in the United States, voluntary sterilization is an even more popular method of birth control for couples over thirty than the pill.[163]

Voluntary sterilization generally is accomplished through performing either a vasectomy[164] on a man or tubal ligation[165] on a woman. Both procedures are considered very safe and, as a rule, irreversible.

In addition to voluntary sterilizations, many states have laws that authorize the involuntary sterilization of certain classes of their citizens — usually inmates of state institutions who are afflicted with certain forms of insanity or mental deficiency.[166]

This section considers a few of the many questions arising out of the performance of both voluntary and involuntary sterilizations.

Availability of Public Assistance to Help Pay Cost of Sterilization Procedure

QUESTION: Are federal funds available to finance the cost of a sterilization procedure?

ANSWER: Federal financial assistance may be available to individuals through the Public Health Service and qualified family planning projects.[167] Mentally competent individuals may qualify for financial assistance if (1) they are at least twenty-one years old when they consent to the procedure; (2) they give their voluntary and informed consent to the procedure; and (3) at least 30 days but not more than 180 days have passed between the date informed consent is given and the date of sterilization.[168] Eligibility requirements are subject to change.

QUESTION: Is state public assistance available to help pay for a sterilization procedure?

ANSWER: Maybe.

Recognizing that birth control is often in the public interest, the state of Oklahoma has provided that its Department of Welfare pay for the cost of an adult male's vasectomy if he is under the age of sixty-five and receiving public assistance.[169] Other such assistance programs may now be offered to citizens of various states, and the reader is encouraged to check with his or her local authorities about the availability of such funds.

Necessity of Spousal Consent

QUESTION: Must an individual notify his or her spouse before undergoing a sterilization procedure?

ANSWER: Yes, in some states.

Currently, some states require by statute, with some exceptions, that an individual obtain their spouse's consent to a sterilization procedure.[170] In addition, case law or opinions of attorney generals in other states have held that spousal consent is required.[171] The reader interested in this area needs to consult with his or her attorney to verify the status of these laws — some of which, it is noted, have already been (or may be) declared unconstitutional by various state or federal courts.[172]

Liability for Failed Sterilization Resulting in Conception

QUESTION: May a parent recover money damages from a physician for a pregnancy which results from a failed sterilization procedure?

ANSWER: This question is, in many respects, virtually identical to the question previously considered in connection with liability which may result from failed contraceptions. As a practical matter, however, doctors who perform sterilization procedures usually secure a release from a patient which, in recognition of the imperfections in the practice of medicine, is intended to bar such lawsuits. These releases might not be effective if the failure is due to medical malpractice. The discussion on wrongful pregnancy below should be consulted.

Sterilization as a Condition of Employment

QUESTION: May an employer adopt an employment policy that requires its fertile women employees to undergo a sterilization procedure in order to keep their jobs that, because of exposure to harmful substances, could either harm a developing fetus or affect the individual's fertility?

ANSWER: This question which identifies an important conflict between the employment rights of fertile women and the rights of their (potential) offspring, has been the subject of much debate. In practice, employers typically would not "require" their employees to be sterilized — they simply would not permit them to hold certain jobs (at which point some employees may "choose" to be sterilized). The Supreme Court will consider this subject in the case of *Auto Workers v. Johnson Controls Inc.*, which is noted in Chapter 4.

Involutary Sterilization of the Mentally Impaired

QUESTION: May a mentally disabled individual be involuntarily sterilized?

ANSWER: In some states, yes.

Many state governments have long sought to regulate (terminate) the procreative rights of their mentally impaired citizens. These "eugenic"[173] laws were intended to enhance the public welfare by seeking to eliminate the opportunity for the "unfit" to have "unfit" children of their own.

Prior to 1927, state courts routinely invalidated these state laws that sought to regulate the involuntary sterilization of mentally impaired individuals. That year, the Supreme Court decided that a Virginia eugenic sterilization statute was constitutionally acceptable. In *Buck v. Bell*,[174] the Court considered the case of Carrie Buck, an eighteen-year-old woman who had been committed to the Virginia State Colony for Epileptics and Feebleminded. Her mother and daughter were both retarded. A petition to sterilize Carrie was brought pursuant to Virginia's compulsory sterilization statute. Virginia had enacted this statute in order to further both the health of the mentally incompetent patient and the general welfare of the state.

The Supreme Court, in upholding the statute's constitutionality, reasoned that Carrie Buck was the "probable potential parent of socially inadequate offspring"[175] and, thus, the decision to sterilize her was not irrational. In a famous and often quoted passage, Justice Oliver Wendell Holmes, Jr., writing the Court's opinion, explained:

> We have seen more than once that the public welfare may call upon its best citizens for their lives. It would be strange if it could not call upon those who already sap the strength of the state for their lesser sacrifices often not felt to be such by those concerned, in order to prevent our society from being swamped with incompetence. *It is better for all the world if instead of waiting to execute degenerate offspring for crime, or let them starve for imbecility, society can prevent those who are manifestly unfit from continuing their kind ... Three generations of imbeciles are enough.*[176]

Interestingly, it has been reported that Dr. Roy Nelson, the director of the Lynchburg Hospital in Virginia, indicated almost fifty years after her voluntary sterilization that Carrie Buck would not be considered retarded by today's standards. He stated that she was sterilized because she was a nineteen-year-old unwed mother whose daughter was "slow" and was, herself, the daughter of a woman thought to be a prostitute.[177] Ironically, it also appears by one account that Carrie Buck's daughter, who was only one month old when diagnosed as "mentally defective" by a nurse, was actually very intelligent.[178] This report emphatically raises the troubling possibility of mistaken diagnoses in the determination to sterilize purported incompetents.

Recognition of this troubling possibility and the finality of a sterilization procedure perhaps explains the apparent retrenchment of the Supreme Court in its later decision on the involuntary sterilization of habitual criminals in the state of Oklahoma. In the case of *Skinner v. Oklahoma,*[179] the Court, in striking down this state's eugenic sterilization statute on equal protection grounds, observed:

> We are dealing here with legislation which involves one of the basic civil rights of man. Marriage and procreation are fundamental to the very existence and survival of the race. The power to sterilize, if exercised, may have subtle, far reaching and devastating effects.... There is no redemption for the individual whom the law touches. Any experiment which the state conducts is to his irreparable injury. He is forever deprived of a basic liberty.[180]

The final chapter on the legality of "forced sterilization," which some states still practice, has surely yet to be written.

Paternity

Introduction

The paternity proceeding appears to have originated in sixteenth century England as a means by which fathers could be forced to provide financial support to thier illegitimate children.[181] The primary purpose of the early English law appears to have been to relieve the local parishes from the expense of supporting illegitimate children and, of lesser significance, to protect the child from the financial and emotional rigors of a life without a father. Many observers would now identify the rights of parents and children as having greater priority than protection of the public coffers.[182]

There are essentially two kinds of paternity proceedings: first, where a suit is filed to establish the paternal obligations of a man who *denies* his paternity; second, where a man brings the suit *to establish* his paternity in order to obtain custody or visitation rights.

There are many far reaching issues which bear upon this subject, including, for example, whether an unmarried father may object to the adoption of his child, and whether a natural father has a right to obtain custody of his child where the mother is deceased. Many of these important questions are beyond the scope of this book. The following brief discussion touches only on two subjects: (1) the means by which paternity may be established and (2) the burdens of proof involved in paternity cases.

Method of Proof

QUESTION: How is paternity established?

ANSWER: Traditionally, paternity has been established (or refuted) by testing the blood and semen of the putative father to see if there is a "matching" with the blood type of the putative child. These types of tests are generally considered 90–95 percent reliable. Recently, a new test called "DNA typing" has been developed by a British geneticist.[183] This test has been described as "unlock[ing] the secrets within DNA, or deoxyribonucleic acid, which carries the genetic information that determines individual characteristics such as eye color and body size."[184] The stated advantage to this test is that unlike traditional blood and semen tests, which typically have an accuracy rating of 90–95 percent, DNA typing is, supporters claim, virtually 100 percent accurate.[185] This means that paternity could soon be conclusively established—or not. Supporters believe that this new test will soon become routine throughout the country.[186]

Burden of Proof

QUESTION: In a paternity proceeding, what is the burden of proof to establish paternity?

ANSWER: In a majority of states, the burden of proof is "by a preponderance of the evidence." A minority of states use a more difficult "clear and convincing" standard. West Virginia uses the most difficult "beyond a reasonable doubt" standard.[187]

Proof by a Preponderance of the Evidence

Most states consider a paternity proceeding to be a "civil," as opposed to a "criminal" proceeding. The reasons for this categorization vary, but often are based on the premise that the purpose of the proceeding is not to punish the father but to prevent the child from becoming a public charge. Accordingly, the burden of proof upon the petitioner in this type of proceeding is the "easier" civil standard of a "preponderance of the evidence"—and not the more difficult criminal standard of proof—proof beyond a reasonable doubt. The standard was adopted by the Pennsylvania Supreme Court in *Minnich v. Rivera,*[188] in which this court explained that in "weighing the standard of proof that should apply in paternity trials, it is incumbent upon [the courts] to (1) appraise the interest of the individual alleged to be the father along with the interests of the child and the mother; (2) assess the commonwealth's interest in family matters and in establishing paternity under a particular standard of proof; and (3) consider the risk that those interests may be erroneously deprived because of the standard applied."[189]

The Pennsylvania court found that consideration of the child's interest in "knowing his father and having two parents to provide and care for him," the mother's interest "in receiving from the child's natural father help, financial and otherwise, in raising and caring for the child born out of wedlock," and the commonwealth's interest in having "its infant citizen having two parents to provide and care for them," justifies use of the lower "proof by a preponderance of the evidence" standard.[190]

Proof by Clear and Convincing Evidence

A small minority of states require a petitioner to meet a higher standard of proof than the preponderance of the evidence standard. In New York, for example, courts hold that "in a paternity proceeding, the burden is on the [petitioner] to establish paternity by "clear and convincing evidence...."[191] This standard seeks to recognize the burdensome consequences to the individual found financially responsible in a paternity proceeding.

Proof Beyond a Reasonable Doubt

Finally, it appears that only West Virginia holds that the appropriate standard of proof in a paternity action is the "beyond a reasonable doubt" criminal standard. In *State ex rel Toryak v. Spagnuolo,*[192] the West Virginia Supreme Court of Appeals observed that once paternity is established in accordance with state law, the defendant's failure to make support payments could subject him to prosecution under the criminal nonsupport statute.[193] These criminal implications, the court held, mandate application of the "proof of paternity beyond a reasonable doubt" standard.[194]

Right to Proof—A Footnote

QUESTION: Do all putative fathers have a "right to prove" a particular child is theirs?

ANSWER: No. Some states statutorily presume that a husband who is living with the child's mother (his wife) at the time of the child's birth and who desires to raise the child as his own is conclusively recognized as the child's father. Accordingly, a man having an affair with a married woman, which results in the birth of a child, may be unable to establish his paternity. The Supreme Court considered—and upheld—the constitutionality of such a presumption in the case of *Michael H. v. Gerald D.*[195]

Rights of the Unborn

Introduction

As the above discussion indicates, many questions that concern the rights and responsibilities associated with reproduction are answered by judicial consideration of a *woman's* right to reproductive freedom. To a typically much lesser extent, courts consider the interested man's rights in seeking to resolve many of the questions. As discussed above, the "right to privacy" has formed the basis for the abortion right, contraception rights, and the right, ordinarily, to be free to procreate as one chooses.

The breadth of these reproductive and privacy rights is not, however, without limitations. In recent years, courts have begun to recognize that a woman's right to privacy and control over her body must be balanced against the right of the fetus she carries while pregnant. This recognition has seen the emergence of a new body of rights: fetal rights. This branch of law concerns such issues as the protection of the fetus from a pregnant mother's drug or alcohol abuse, medical emergencies that result when a pregnant woman refuses certain medical treatment that jeopardizes the health and well-being of the fetus, and the infliction of injuries on the fetus — both prior to birth and, in some instances, prior to conception. As part of the emergence of "fetal rights," claims have been asserted and given serious consideration by some courts — that individuals may have a right not to have been born at all. This section reviews some of the many interesting and critical issues in the emerging field of "fetal rights" — the rights of the unborn.

Protection of Fertilized Embryos

Protection from Intentional Destruction

QUESTION: Are embryos produced by in vitro fertilization protected from intentional destruction?

ANSWER: This novel question was recently considered by a Tennessee trial court, which held that such embryos are protected.

A much publicized case in Tennessee recently considered what is believed to be an unprecedented legal issue: how to dispose of embryos produced by in vitro fertilization for a divorced couple when one spouse seeks to have the embryos destroyed and the other spouse seeks permission to bring the embryos to term through implantation in her womb.

Davis v. Davis[196] considered the fate of seven embryos that had been suspended in liquid nitrogen in the East Tennessee Fertility Center in Knoxville, Tennessee. The embryos were developed in December 1988, from Ms. Davis' eggs and Mr. Davis' sperm. When the couple's divorce proceedings commenced, the fate of these embryos became uncertain. Mr. Davis sought to have the embryos destroyed because, as he testified, he did not want any child of his to be raised in a single-parent home, as he had been. He also alleged that "[t]hey are going to force me to become a father against my wishes."[197] Ms. Davis, who has had five tubal pregnancies, was advised by her physicians that it would be dangerous for her to attempt to give birth to a normally conceived child. She believed that the in vitro fertilization of these embryos was "kind of [her] last hope."[198]

The Tennessee trial court, holding that these seven embryos were human beings and not property, ruled in favor of Ms. Davis. The court explained that by proceeding with the laboratory fertilization, "Mr. and Mrs. Davis have produced human beings . . . to be known as their child or children."[199] The court reasoned that "it served the best interests of the child or children, in vitro, for their mother . . . to be permitted the opportunity to bring them to term through implantation" in her womb.[200]

Mr. Davis indicated immediately after the trial court's decision that he would seek a "stay of implantation" and appeal the decision to a higher court. It remains to be seen how this unusual legal issue will be resolved in the Tennessee appellate courts and other states that might face similar cases in the future. It appears that Louisiana is the only state that has, to date, specifically addressed this issue by legislation, that being a statute enacted in 1986 that prohibits embryos from being intentionally destroyed or sold.[201]

Protection from Drug and Alcohol Abuse

QUESTION: Are unborn children protected from their pregnant mother's drug and alcohol abuse?
ANSWER: Pregnant women are increasingly placed at risk of civil and criminal penalties if they abuse drugs or alcohol.

It is now generally recognized that drug, alcohol, and tobacco use during pregnancy may impair proper fetal development. New terms, such as "fetal tobacco syndrome,"[202] are being used to identify some of the problems caused by use of such substances. The law is becoming increasingly intolerant of pregnant women who abuse drugs, alcohol, or tobacco to the injury of the developing fetus. States across the country are beginning to utilize their criminal law in order to hold these pregnant women responsible for their victims.

Recently, a Florida court found a mother guilty of two felony counts of delivering cocaine to her newborn babies through the umbilical cord.[203] The mother now faces up to thirty years in prison for each felony charge. In this case, the mother gave birth to a baby in 1987 and another baby in 1989. Both babies were born with cocaine derivatives in their systems. Although Florida law does not recognize the fetus as a person, the prosecution was able to focus on a short period of time after the children were born but before the umbilical cord was cut (between sixty and ninety seconds after birth) during which time, experts testified, the mother, who had smoked crack cocaine only hours before giving birth, actually delivered the drug to her infants through the umbilical cord.[204] A Florida prosecutor explained that the purpose of this proceeding was not to incarcerate the mother but to prevent child abuse.

In what may be the first action of its kind in the country, a woman has been charged in Illinois with involuntary manslaughter (and delivery of a controlled substance) after her two-day-old baby daughter, born with cocaine in her system, died.[205] An autopsy revealed that the mother's drug use had reduced the baby's oxygen supply, which led to fatal brain damage after her birth.[206] The district attorney in this case explained that "this is not a right to life or fetal right's case, it's the rights of an infant . . . [w]hat we're doing is protecting children."[207]

Although the extent to which criminal laws across the country will be used to protect children remains to be seen, it is a safe bet to assume that pregnant women who abuse alcohol or drugs to the detriment of their fetuses may become increasingly subject to stiff criminal penalties.

In addition to incarcerating substance abusers for violation of criminal laws, courts are also beginning to regulate a pregnant woman's lifestyle during the course of her pregnancy when evidence of substance abuse is established. For example, an Illinois court ordered a pregnant woman, who had previously given birth to a heroin-addicted child, to refrain from using heroin during the course of another pregnancy.[208]

In another case, a Baltimore court required a pregnant woman, who had previously given birth to a drug-addicted child, to enter a drug rehabilitation program and submit to weekly urinalysis for the entire term of her pregnancy.[209]

Legal Action against Drug and Alcohol Suppliers for Injuries Caused to a Developing Fetus

QUESTION: May the parents of a child who has suffered birth defects as a result of the mother's abuse of alcohol or drugs during her pregnancy recover damages from the supplier of drugs or alcohol who fails to warn of the risk of such defects?

ANSWER: Traditionally, such claims have not been recognized, but the law is developing and such claims may begin to find recognition.

There is very little case law on the subject of whether parents of a child who has suffered birth defects as a result of the mother's alcohol or drug abuse may sue the supplier of such drugs or alcohol. This area will likely be a source of increased litigation in the future. It is noted that in what has been described as the "first such suit [of its] kind in the country to go to trial" a Washington couple, in a suit captioned *Thorp v. James B. Beam Distilling Co.,* brought an action against a bourbon manufacturer on the ground that it had an obligation to warn consumers when it learned in 1978 that pregnant women who drink alcohol could produce children with birth defects.[210]

In *Thorp,* the plaintiff's suit against the bourbon manufacturer alleged that the mother's drinking caused her four-year-old son to be born mentally retarded, as well as with physical malformations.[211] The mother, who admitted to being an alcoholic, conceded that she drank as much as half a fifth per day of bourbon while she was pregnant.[212] The mother further alleged that she did not know her drinking would cause birth defects to her son. The plaintiffs claimed that the bourbon manufacturer should have provided labels on the alcohol bottles which warned that alcohol use by pregnant women could cause birth defects. The defendant asserted that the mother had been warned repeatedly by family members and doctors that alcohol could produce birth defects, and that "a warning on the bottle label would not have done any good."[213] A Seattle jury ruled that the defendant was not liable for the child's birth defects.[214] Although this decision may slow down the commencement of similar types of lawsuits, others will surely follow and attempt to establish an alcohol manufacturer or drug supplier's liability for causally related birth defects. It remains to be seen whether such claims will find success.

Regulation of a Woman's Diet during Pregnancy

QUESTION: May a court of law regulate a pregnant woman's diet in order to prevent a perceived harm to her fetus?

ANSWER: Possibly.

Although there is relatively little legal authority concerning this issue, some courts have, under extreme circumstances, stood ready to regulate a pregnant woman's diet for the protection of the fetus. A California court considered a request to prohibit a woman from following a dangerous fad diet (under which she could only eat organic foods) from conceiving children as a condition of her probation on a previous conviction for child endangerment.[215] Although the court rejected this proposed condition, it did hold that if the woman became pregnant, she would be "required to follow an intensive prenatal and neonatal treatment program monitored by both the probation officer and by a supervising physician."[216]

Medical Emergencies

The subject of fetal rights also continues to be developing in the area of "medical emergencies." Probably the most important question running throughout this area of law is whether the government, doctors, or interested third parties may force a pregnant woman to undergo medical treatment, including by surgical invasion of her body, against her wishes, for what they perceive to be action which is in the best interests of the developing fetus.

This section addresses such questions as whether a pregnant woman may be forcibly subjected to medical treatment such as blood transfusions or to a cesarean section delivery, against her will, if deemed necessary for the unborn child's survival or healthy development by her obstetrician.

> QUESTION: In a medical emergency, may a pregnant woman be compelled to have a cesarean section operation during labor and delivery over her objection?
>
> ANSWER: In a medical emergency, a pregnant woman may be compelled to undergo such an operation.

Although this area of law is continuing to develop, there is case precedent that supports the proposition that a pregnant woman may be compelled to undergo a cesarean section operation in a medical emergency. One of the earliest recorded decisions involved a woman in labor who, upon arriving at a Denver hospital, showed signs of fetal distress.[217] Although her physicians proposed a cesarean section, she refused, apparently, in part, because she was obese and the procedure was risky as a result.[218] A hospital psychiatrist examined the woman and concluded that she was mentally competent to decide not to undergo the surgery. The hospital attorneys thereafter sought a court order authorizing performance of the cesarean section. In a hearing held at the woman's bedside, a Denver Juvenile Court judge declared the fetus neglected and, relying on a Colorado statute that authorizes medical treatment to a neglected child when in the best interest of a child,[219] ordered the operation performed. The court also relied on the states *parens patriae* authority in holding that it had the power to provide the fetus with medical treatment over the parents' "unreasonable" objection.[220] It is interesting to note that the decision in this case to require the cesarean operation was based on an erroneous reading of the fetal monitor concerning the possible damage to the fetus if birth was delayed.[221]

Other examples of judicial decisions in this area highlight the grave public policy issues at stake when the legal system seeks to override the pregnant woman's decision on whether or not to undergo medical treatment. In 1982, a Michigan judge, concerned about possible complications to a fetus, entered an order requiring a pregnant woman to be picked up and transported to a hospital by the local police if she did not voluntarily admit herself there by a specified time.[222] The judge's order further directed her to submit to "whatever the medical personnel deemed appropriate including a cesarean section and medication."[223] The woman then fled and, while in hiding, gave an uncomplicated vaginal birth to a healthy baby.[224]

Finally, it is important to recognize that all cases which have raised this question have *not* resulted in a court ordering a forced cesarean operation.

In a state of Washington case,[225] social services attorneys sought a court order compelling a pregnant woman, who had tested positive for herpes, to undergo a cesarean section. The attorneys were apparently concerned that the herpes would be transmitted to the child by a vaginal delivery. The judge refused to order the operation, stating, "I just don't feel that the state has the power to require a parent to undergo . . . what I consider a major surgical procedure—and I use the term 'major' because it does require anesthetic and there are certain risks in any . . . surgical procedures. . . ."[226]

> QUESTION: If a pregnant woman needs a blood transfusion, may she be compelled to have such a transfusion over her objection?
>
> ANSWER: Probably yes.

The leading case precedent in this area is *Raleigh Fitkin-Paul Morgan Memorial Hospital v. Anderson*.[227] This case concerned a Jehovah's Witness who in her eighth month of pregnancy and while hospitalized was advised to undergo blood transfusions. The woman objected to the transfusions for religious reasons. The court ordered the patient notwithstanding her objection, to undergo the transfusions. The court identified two critical issues: (1) a fetus' right to medical treatment and (2) compelling an adult to submit to medical procedures she chooses not to have.[228] The court, after noting that the state had an interest in preserving fetal life, chose not to decide the second issue because "the welfare of the child and the mother are so intertwined and inseparable that it would be impractical to attempt to distinguish them."[229] Interestingly, after the woman was ordered to undergo a blood transfusion, she left the hospital and, later, delivered a healthy child without having had the transfusion. Obviously this result again raises the difficult question of who really knows what is in a child's — or fetus' — best interest.

In *Hoener v. Bertinato*,[230] a New Jersey court considered whether a pregnant woman who was a Jehovah's Witness, could be ordered to permit her child to have a blood transfusion immediately after her child's birth in order to address a blood condition which could otherwise, her doctors testified, have caused the child to die.[231]

This court first noted that while laws "cannot constitutionally interfere with mere *religious beliefs* and opinions, they may interfere with *religious practices* inconsistent with the peace and safety of the state — here, the protection of the lives and health of its children."[232]

In concluding that the state could exercise its "parens patriae" authority to order the transfusion for a child not yet born, the court found that "[s]ince the blood transfusions are required in order for the child to live, the [parents'] refusal to consent thereto constitutes 'neglect to provide the child with proper protection' under the [New Jersey child neglect] statute."[233]

> QUESTION: May a pregnant woman be compelled against her wishes to submit to surgery to maintain and preserve the pregnancy prior to the fetus' viability?
> ANSWER: Probably not.

It appears that *prior to a fetus' viability,* states will generally *not* interfere with a pregnant woman's decision in this regard and will not compel them to undergo surgery that may save a fetus. This position, probably is based, at least in part, on a recognition of a pregnant woman's right, under certain circumstances, to have an abortion. In *Taft v. Taft*,[234] the Massachusetts Supreme Court considered a lower state court order which required a pregnant woman to submit to a suturing operation to prevent the miscarriage of her not yet viable fetus in spite of her objection to the operation on religious grounds. The lower court, noting that the woman had previously required this surgical procedure to carry her other children to term, found that this operation was a "very minor one" and ordered its performance.[235] The Massachusetts Supreme Court, on appeal, reversed the lower court's decision and upheld the woman's refusal to submit to the operation.[236] Although the court recognized the state's interest in the well-being of unborn children,[237] it held that such interest could not override the woman's right to practice her religion as she chose.[238] The court then observed that some situations might justify mandatory medical treatment to sustain the completion of a pregnancy.[239]

Wrongful Pregnancy

QUESTION: What is meant by the term "wrongful pregnancy"?

ANSWER: It typically refers to the situation where an unplanned or unwanted pregnancy results due to a third party's negligence.

QUESTION: What kind of negligence can give rise to a claim for wrongful pregnancy?

ANSWER: Typical "wrongful pregnancy" claims involve (1) claims of negligently performed tubal ligations; (2) negligently performed vasectomies; (3) negligently filled birth control prescriptions; (4) negligently manufactured condoms; (5) failure to reinsert contraceptive device following routine medical examination; (6) failure to timely diagnose pregnancy and thereby foreclosing the abortion option; and (7) negligently performing an abortion.

QUESTION: Do state courts recognize these claims?

ANSWER: It appears that most courts do recognize the validity of these claims.

It appears that most state courts that have considered wrongful pregnancy claims have determined that this "category" of claim is legitimate and may, under appropriate circumstances, justify the imposition of money damages against the "responsible" party. The broad acceptance of the wrongful pregnancy action probably stems from its similarity to a traditional medical malpractice action (for instance, a negligently performed sterilization) or a traditional "products liability action" (for instance, the improper manufacture of a condom).[240]

Not all courts, however, recognize wrongful pregnancy claims. For example, in *Schork v. Huber*,[241] the Kentucky Supreme Court rejected the claim of parents seeking the cost of raising a healthy child. In this case, the mother had undergone a sterilization procedure performed by the defendant physician. After the procedure was completed, the defendant advised the woman that she was sterile. She thereafter experienced what she believed to be a miscarriage but the defendant, without performing any tests, again advised her that she was sterile. Several months later the plaintiff became pregnant and later delivered a healthy boy.[242]

The parents then brought a lawsuit against the doctor to recover damages for medical malpractice, the costs of raising the child, damages for disruption of family life, and mental suffering.[243]

In deciding that the parents could not recover the costs of raising the unplanned child, the Kentucky Supreme Court stated:

> The parents of a normal healthy child whom they now love have not suffered any injury or damage. The benefits conferred by the child's existence clearly outweigh any economic burden involved. The claimed injury is far too speculative and remote to be reasonably connected to the negligence. Additionally, in a pure legal sense the parents [by failing to have an abortion?] have failed to mitigate the damages which they charge....
>
> That a child can be considered as an injury offends fundamental concepts attached to human life.[244]

QUESTION: In states that do recognize the validity of this type of claim, what damages can be recovered in a successful suit?

ANSWER: Typically, damages for (1) pain and suffering incurred during pregnancy and childbirth; (2) medical expenses incurred as a result of pregnancy and delivery; and (3) lost wages are recoverable. In addition, if the claim arises as a result of a negligently performed tubal ligation or vasectomy, the cost of the original procedure — may also be recovered. Finally, there is a case precedent that holds that if parents choose to abort the unplanned pregnancy, the costs of the abortion would also be recoverable.[245]

QUESTION: Are the costs of raising an unplanned child also recoverable?

ANSWER: The answer to this question varies from state to state. No case has been located in which a state court has allowed parents to recover the full cost of raising unplanned children although some decisions could be construed to authorize such recovery in the proper circumstances. Some states permit the recovery of the costs of upbringing the unplanned child and "offset" the value of the emotional benefits parents will derive from their children. Some states refuse to permit any recovery for such costs.

Majority Rule — Costs of Raising Unplanned Children Are Not Recoverable

It seems that the vast majority of state courts that have been asked to consider the issue of whether the costs of raising unplanned children are recoverable in wrongful pregnancy cases have sided with the defendants and have rejected such claims.[246] These courts generally reason, as did the court in *Schork v. Huber,* discussed above, that parents are not "injured" or "damaged" by the birth of a normal, healthy child.[247]

A federal court for the District of Columbia, adopting the majority rule, has indicated that, in accordance with the general principle that an injured party must take steps to mitigate (reduce) her damages, a woman who becomes "wrongfully pregnant" could either have an abortion or place the unwanted child up for adoption.[248] Either one of these steps, it reasoned, would eliminate the claim for the costs of raising an unwanted child.

Minority Rule — Balance of Benefits

A second approach has been adopted by some courts that have been forced to grapple with the extent of damages in a wrongful pregnancy case. This approach generally permits the parents of an unplanned child to recover the costs of upbringing the child (through to the age of majority) less the value of the emotional benefits plaintiffs will receive in their role as parents.[249] Courts that adopt this approach leave damages computations to the jury to determine, believing that jurors are capable of handling the obviously speculative nature of the damages involved in such types of claims.[250] Often, the parents' reasons for bringing the claim is considered the most telling evidence of whether or to what extent the birth of the child actually injured the parents. For example, parents who sought to avoid the pregnancy because of fears of genetic birth defects are less likely to be able to show a greater burden than a benefit if their fears prove unfounded. Proof that economic factors motivated the parent's choice to avoid conception might establish that the burdens of the unplanned child's birth outweighs the benefits.[251]

This approach was adopted by the Maryland Court of Appeals in *Jones v. Malinowski*.[252] In this case, parents brought an action against a physician who had negligently performed a sterilization procedure on the woman (by failing to identify and block the left fallopian tube).[253] As a result of the failed procedure, the parents gave birth to a healthy girl.

The parents, who had limited financial resources, sued the doctor for having placed a greater financial burden on them, by having to rear an unexpected child.[254] Evidence indicated that it would cost the parents between approximately $50,000 and $85,000 to raise the unplanned child from birth to maturity.[255] The jury awarded damages to the parents in the amount of $70,000[256] The doctor appealed the decision arguing that the costs of childrearing could not be considered as an element of the parents' damages.[257]

The Maryland Appellate Court determined that the jury may properly award damages to parents that *include* childrearing costs to the age of majority, as long as these damages are "offset by the benefits derived by the parents from the child's aid, society and comfort."[258] In calculating this offset, the court explained that "[t]he jury must assess these benefits in light of the circumstances of the particular case under consideration, taking into account, among other things, family size and income, age of the parents and other relevant factors...."[259] The court then affirmed the jury's award of $70,000 to the plaintiffs in this case.[260]

Minority Rule — Full Recovery Permitted

A small minority of cases, recognizing the generally accepted legal principle that a wrongdoer is liable for all foreseeable harm of his wrongful conduct, have suggested — but not clearly decided — that parents may recover all of the costs of raising an unplanned child in a successful wrongful pregnancy claim.

In *Custodio v. Bauer*,[261] the California Court of Appeals considered the claim of parents who sought to recover damages resulting from an unsuccessful sterilization operation which resulted in the birth of an unwanted child. The plaintiffs sought recovery for (1) the medical expenses (and pain) of the failed operation; (2) mental pain incident

to the pregnancy; and (3) the economic expenses caused by the unwanted child.

The court, holding that the plaintiffs were entitled to recover all damages proximately caused by the doctor's negligence, stated that "[w]here
the mother survives without casualty there is still some loss. She must
spread her society, comfort, care, protection and support over a larger
group. If this change in the family status can be measured economically,
it should be . . . compensable. . . ."[262]

In this case, the California appellate court indicated that it could
not, on the record before it, determine the actual amount of damages
suffered by the plaintiffs. The court noted, however, that "[i]t is clear
that if successful on the issue of liability, [the plaintiffs] have established
a right to *more than nominal damages.*"[263] Some later California decisions may have retreated from this position in favor of the "balance of
benefits rule," discussed above.

In *Bowman v. Davis,*[264] the plaintiff delivered healthy twins following a negligently performed tubal ligation by the defendant, the doctor
who performed the ligation. After a jury awarded the plaintiff $450,000,
the defendant appealed, arguing that both public policy and the plaintiff's
signature on a consent form, signed prior to the operation, should bar the
plaintiff's recovery of damages.[265] The Ohio Supreme Court upheld the
jury award on the grounds that (1) public policy favored the plaintiff
(who enjoyed the constitutional right not to procreate) and (2) the consent form which the plaintiff signed applied to situations where the tubal
ligation was effective and the plaintiff, thereafter, might attempt to
establish that she was unaware of the operation's permanent effect.[266] It
should be noted that the Ohio Supreme Court observed that the defendants had not argued that the plaintiff's recovery should be limited to only
the expenses of pregnancy—and so, it indicated that it was not deciding
that point (although it probably could have done so on its own).[267]

In short, no case has been found in which a jurisdiction has clearly
adopted the "full-recovery" rule.

Wrongful Life

QUESTION: What is meant by the term "wrongful life"?
ANSWER: It generally refers to a claim that the defendant breached
           a duty to inform prospective parents of certain hazards
           which ultimately result in the birth of an impaired child.

QUESTION: Who brings a wrongful life claim?
ANSWER: The claim is brought on behalf of the impaired child. [The parents may also bring a "companion" claim for wrongful pregnancy, discussed above.]

QUESTION: Who is the claim typically brought against?
ANSWER: A doctor or other member of the medical community who improperly renders poor prenatal care or counseling which "results" in the birth of the impaired child — instead of that child's abortion while still a fetus.

QUESTION: Do state courts recognize this type of claim?
ANSWER: Although not universally recognized, some states are now beginning to recognize the validity of at least some elements of this type of claim.

QUESTION: Why have some states failed to recognize this type of claim?
ANSWER: Courts which have rejected wrongful life claims have done so for a variety of reasons. These reasons are discussed below.

Wrongful Life Claims Are Offensive to Public Policy

The most frequent reason offered for rejecting a claim for wrongful life is that it would offend public policy to hold one has a legal right not to be born when the overriding policy of the state is to protect and preserve human life. For example, in *Elliott v. Brown,*[268] the Alabama Supreme Court explained, in a passage worth quoting at length, that

> Fundamental to the recognition of such a cause of action is the notion that the defendant has violated some legal right of plaintiff's and as a result she has suffered injury. However, *a legal right not to be born is alien to the public policy of this State to protect and preserve human life.* The right of women in certain cases to have abortions does not alter the policy. Instead, in light of this right the recognition of such a cause of action raises more questions than it answers. In the words of one jurist:
>
>> "...Implicit, beyond this claim against a physician for faulty advice, is the proposition that a pregnant woman who, duly informed, does not seek an abortion, and all who urge her to see the pregnancy through are guilty of wrongful injury to the fetus, and indeed that every day in which the infant is sustained after birth is a day of wrong. *To recognize a right not to be born is to enter*

*an area in which no one could find his way." Gleitman v.
Cosgrove,* 227 A.2d at 711 (Weintraub, C.J., dissenting in part).

We hold that there is no legal right not to be born and the plaintiff has
no cause of action for "wrongful life."[269]

Wrongful Life Claims Seek Damages
That Are Impossible to Measure

Another frequent reason offered for rejecting a wrongful life claim
is that it would be impossible, when seeking to measure the amount of
a child's damages for having been born, to determine the difference in
value of an impaired life versus no life at all. For example, in *Dumer v.
St. Michael's Hospital,*[270] the supreme court of Wisconsin considered
the case of a woman who sought treatment for an upper body rash in
the defendant hospital's emergency room. Although the woman believed
she had rubella, and suggested this possibility to the treating physician,
the physican negligently diagnosed her condition as an allergic reac-
tion.[271] The physician discharged the woman, who, at the time, was one
month pregnant. The woman later gave birth to a baby who suffered
from physical and mental retardation, cataracts, and heart malfunc-
tion.[272]

The mother then brought suit on her behalf and her child's behalf,
claiming that the physician's failure to diagnose rubella, and advise the
mother of the possible effects of rubella on the fetus, and the possibility
of an abortion, prevented the child from being aborted, contributed to
her personal injury and to the financial injury of her parents.[273]

The Wisconsin court, in considering the infant's claim for wrongful
life (i.e. that she should not have been allowed to be born and her birth
has left her permanently unable to enjoy life) stated:

> The infant plaintiff is therefore required to say not that he should have
> been born without defects but that he should not have been born at all.
> In the language of tort law he says: but for the negligence of defen-
> dants, he would not have been born to suffer with an impaired body.
> In other words, he claims that the conduct of defendants prevented his
> mother from obtaining an abortion which would have terminated his
> existence, and that his very life is "wrongful."
>
> The normal measure of damages in tort actions is compensatory.
> Damages are measured by comparing the condition plaintiff would
> have been in, had the defendants not been negligent, with plaintiff's

impaired condition as a result of the negligence. *The infant plaintiff would have us measure the difference between his life with defects against the utter void of nonexistence, but it is impossible to make such a determination. This Court cannot weigh the value of life with impairments against the nonexistence of life itself.* By asserting that he should not have been born, the infant plaintiff makes it logically impossible for a court to measure his alleged damages because of the impossibility of making the comparison required by compensatory remedies.[274]

QUESTION: What rationale has been offered by those courts which have recognized some aspects of a cause of action for wrongful life?

ANSWER: No decision has been uncovered which expressly permits an action for wrongful life. Instead, some decisions have indicated a willingness to authorize recovery of damages to pay for the costs of treating the birth defects an impaired child may need.

In *Procanik v. Cielo,*[275] the New Jersey Supreme Court considered the case of a woman who, during the first trimester of pregnancy, consulted with the defendant to determine whether or not she had contracted rubella.[276] The defendant mistakenly advised the plaintiff that she did not have this disease. Based on this advice, the mother chose not to have an abortion and her child was born with multiple congenital defects, including heart disease and eye lesions.[277]

In considering this case, the New Jersey court emphasized that the child would require extraordinary medical care, the financial impact of which would be felt by both the parents and the child.[278] In this case, in which the *parents'* right to recover for medical expenses to treat their child's blindness, deafness, and retardation was barred by the statute of limitations, the court found that the *child* could recover such expenses, in his own right, because such expenses were reasonably certain and readily calculable.[279]

Wrongful Infliction of Prenatal Injuries

QUESTION: What is meant by the term "prenatal tort"?

ANSWER: A prenatal tort refers to wrongful conduct by an individual or entity that, occurring after another individual's conception but prior to birth, results in injuries to that other individual.

QUESTION: Do courts recognize prenatal torts and allow recovery
of money damages by the injured individuals?

ANSWER: Although for many years courts denied recovery for
prenatal torts, such claims are now generally recognized
throughout the United States.

Justice Oliver Wendell Holmes and the Supreme Court of Massachusetts first considered a claim for prenatal torts in *Dietrich v. Inhabitants of Northampton*.[280] In this case, a pregnant woman suffered a miscarriage when she tripped on a negligently maintained highway. The woman thereafter brought suit on behalf of the miscarried fetus. Justice Holmes, writing the court's opinion, denied any claim for injuries sustained before birth.[281]

The *Dietrich* precedent stood for many years but, as science advanced, its logic was gradually eroded.

The erosion finally gave way to what has been described as one of the most "abrupt reversal(s) of a well settled rule" in the history of torts.[282] This reversal began with a federal district court's decisions in the case of *Bonbrest v. Kotz,*[283] which recognized "the law is presumed to keep pace with the sciences and medical science certainly has made progress since [*Dietrich*] was decided."[284] Accordingly, the court chose to recognize that "a child, if born alive and viable, should be allowed to maintain an action in the courts for injuries wrongfully committed upon its person while in the womb of its mother."[285]

QUESTION: Must a fetus be viable[286] in order to be entitled to
recover for prenatal torts?

ANSWER: Not necessarily.

Although the *Bonbrest* decision limited recovery for prenatal torts to injuries caused to a viable fetus, this standard soon gave way to decisions which recognized an individual's right to recover for prenatal injuries which occurred prior to that individual's viability. One of the first cases recognizing this right was *Kelly v. Gregory*.[287] In this case, a New York appellate court, finding that the viability requirement was a "highly artificial distinction [in] law," held that if a child born after injury sustained at *any* period of his prenatal life can prove the effect of a tort on him, recovery should be allowed.[288]

Wrongful Infliction of Preconception Injuries

QUESTION: What is meant by the term "preconception tort"?

ANSWER: A preconception tort refers to wrongful conduct by an individual or entity that, occurring prior to another individual's conception, results in injuries to that other individual. (This differs from a prenatal tort, discussed above, which involves a tortious act committed after the individual's conception but before his birth.)

QUESTION: Do courts recognize preconception torts and allow recovery of money damages by the injured individual?

ANSWER: To date, only several courts have recognized the validity of a claim for injuries caused to an individual prior to that individual's conception. Most courts that have considered such claims have denied recovery.

One of the first judicial decisions that addressed — and upheld — a claim for the wrongful infliction of preconception injuries is *Renslow v. Mennonite Hospital.*[289] In this case, the supreme court of Illinois, finding that a physician's negligent transfusion of Rh-negative blood into a woman who had Rh-positive blood caused birth defects to her child born several years later, stated that it was "illogical to bar relief for an act done prior to conception where the defendant would be liable for this same conduct had the child, unbeknownst to him, been conceived prior to his act. We believe that there is a right to be born free from prenatal injuries foreseeably caused by a breach of duty to the child's mother."[290]

Most courts, however, have yet to recognize the validity of a claim for injuries caused to an individual prior to that individual's conception. For example, a New York appellate court held in *Albala v. City of New York*[291] that an individual did not have a right to recover for injuries resulting from a tort committed against his mother prior to his conception. In this case, the plaintiff's mother underwent an abortion in 1971. The abortion was negligently performed and resulted in the perforation of the mother's uterus.[292] The mother thereafter settled a malpractice suit for $175,000 against the physician who performed the abortion. Almost four years after the negligently performed abortion, the plaintiff was conceived.[293] The plaintiff's suit alleged that as a result of the doctor's previous malpractice with respect to his mother, he had suffered brain damage.[294]

The New York Supreme Court, Appellate Division, rejected the infant's claim for injuries, stating that it was up to the state legislature to create a new cause of action such as this.[295]

Most state legislatures have not accepted this invitation.

Fetal Rights in the Workplace

In some employment situations, thorny questions are raised that implicate a woman's right to hold a job and, at the same time, her developing fetus' right to be protected from hazards in the workplace which could result in birth defects. This subject is discussed in Chapter 4.

Chapter III

Wrongful Transmission of Sexual Diseases

Introduction

Every year, millions of people become infected with painful, sometimes deadly, sexually transmitted diseases. Many of these people contract these diseases from their lovers who deceive them into believing that it would be safe to have sex with them when, in fact, it is not. Increasingly, many victims of sexually transmitted diseases are turning to the legal system to seek monetary compensation and, understandably, revenge against their deceptive lovers. The publicity surrounding the case Mark Christian brought against the estate of his former lover, Rock Hudson, who died from AIDS in 1985, will surely prompt more victims to consider suing their deceptive lovers. Mark Christian's case is especially noteworthy because although he had not contracted AIDS at the time of trial, he argued that, as a result of his love affair with Rock Hudson, who did not disclose that he had AIDS to Christian, he suffered grave emotional distress that he too would contract AIDS and die. For his emotional distress, a Los Angeles jury awarded Christian a stunning $21.75 million in damages in February 1989.[1]

This chapter addresses some of the legal claims that can be made by victims of sexually transmitted diseases against their deceptive lovers. Defenses to these claims that might be available to the individual charged with transmitting a sexual disease are also considered.

Background

QUESTION: What is herpes and how is it transmitted?
ANSWER: Genital herpes, scientifically known as herpes simplex

61

virus type II (HS-II), is a virus typified by recurring breakouts of blisterlike sores on or around the genitals. Genital herpes is highly contagious when in an active state and is usually transmitted through direct contact with a lover's infected secretions. Although the disease is generally considered non–life-threatening, it can be very traumatic. The disease often manifests itself by the recurrent appearance of painful lesions or open sores on the penis in men and the vulva, cervix, or vagina in women. The lesions often heal within six to ten days.[2] Apart from the open sores, genital herpes also can cause itching, pain on urination, fever and headaches. Recurring episodes of genital herpes has been causally linked to the outbreak of such diseases as urethral and bladder infections and aseptic meningitis. Genital herpes continues to spread rapidly throughout the United States.

QUESTION: What is AIDS and how is it transmitted?

ANSWER: AIDS is a shorthand reference for acquired immunodeficiency syndrome. It is now believed that this disease is initiated by a virus known as human immunodeficiency virus (HIV). The virus attacks white blood cells that are necessary for a person's immune system to fight off disease. It is estimated that between 1 and 2 million individuals in the United States alone carry the HIV virus and are capable of spreading that virus. Because it is possible to carry the HIV virus without developing symptoms of AIDS, it is probable that many carriers transmit the virus without being aware of the transmission.

Currently, the vast majority of individuals with AIDS in the United States fall into the following categories: (1) gay or bisexual men; (2) intravenous drug users; (3) recipients of blood transfusions prior to 1983 (when it became possible to screen for the HIV virus in blood); and (4) hemophiliacs.

The mortality associated with AIDS is extremely high. Although worldwide research is being conducted to develop a treatment for AIDS, no generally accepted treatment has yet been developed.

AIDS can be transmitted through heterosexual intercourse.

QUESTION: What are other common diseases that are sexually transmitted?

ANSWER: There are many other diseases which may be transmitted through sexual contact. These include, for example, gonorrhea, syphilis, acute pelvic inflammatory disease and vaginitis.

Claims Against the Transmitting Party

QUESTION: Have courts imposed financial liability on individuals who transmit sexual diseases?

ANSWER: Yes. In some cases, the financial liability imposed can be substantial. Mark Christian's suit against Rock Hudson, noted above, is probably the most publicly recognized example of the imposition of financial liability on a transmitting party for the wrongful transmission of a sexual disease.

 The transmitting party need not be famous, however, to be slapped with a stiff judgment for damages. For example, in one recent case, a woman was awarded $2.1 million against her deceased former husband's estate because of his failure to disclose his gay sexual activities to her. She contacted the HIV virus from her husband who died of AIDS.[3]

QUESTION: What is the basis for the imposition of such liability?

ANSWER: Justification for the imposition of liability is typically based on one or more of the following legal theories: (a) negligence; (b) deceit; (c) assault and battery; and (d) the intentional infliction of emotional distress. The elements of liability are discussed below.

QUESTION: Does it make a difference which of these theories of liability is used by the innocent party seeking damages?

ANSWER: Possibly. Claims based on intentional wrongdoing (i.e., deceit, assault and battery, and the intentional infliction of emotional distress) may justify the imposition of punitive damages (on top of compensatory damages) against the responsible party. In addition, successful proof of an intentional wrong might make otherwise applicable defenses to claims brought for the unintentional (yet negligent) transmission of a disease — which are discussed below — unavailable.

Negligence

QUESTION: What are the traditional elements of a legal cause of action based on an individual defendant's negligence?

ANSWER: Generally, a claim seeking compensation for another
                party's negligence must establish:

                1. A *duty* on the part of the defendant to act in such a
                   manner for the protection of others against unrea-
                   sonable risk of injury;
                2. The defendant's *failure to act reasonably under the
                   circumstances;*
                3. There is a satisfactorily *close causal connection* be-
                   tween the defendant's unreasonable conduct and the
                   resulting injury to the injured party; and
                4. *Actual injury* (not merely fear of injury) resulting
                   to that party.[4]

Many courts appear prepared to impose liability for the transmission of a sexual disease caused by a responsible party's negligent conduct. For example, in *Long v. Adams,*[5] the plaintiff and defendant, who
were unmarried, were involved in an intimate sexual relationship as a
result of which the plaintiff allegedly contracted genital herpes from the
defendant. The plaintiff's suit charged that the defendant infected him
with the disease making her liable to him for money damages as a result.
The plaintiff alleged that the defendant's transmission of the disease to
him constituted negligence, battery, and the intentional infliction of
emotional distress.

After noting the necessary elements for a cause of action founded
on negligence, the court considered what legal duty, if any, is owed by
one sexually active person to another. The court decided that "[t]he duty
owed is the same one that every individual in this state owes another: the
duty to exercise ordinary care not to injure others."[6]

The court also noted that it was "not stating here that herpes' victims have a specific duty to warn any person of their condition; however,
they, like all citizens, are to be guided by those considerations which
ordinarily regulate the conduct of human affairs, and they may be sued
in this State for negligence [for] the omission to do something which a
reasonable person would do."[7]

In response to the defendant's contention that the parties' consensual sex violated the state criminal fornication statute, and so should
bar plaintiff's recovery (which, as noted below, has elsewhere been raised
successfully as a defense to claims such as this), the court explained:

> The theory upon which an injured party is debarred of the right to
> recover when injured while engaged in the performance of an illegal

> or criminal act rests, not upon the ground that he is performing an il-
> legal or criminal act, either alone or jointly with the defendant, but
> upon the ground that his conduct is negligent and is the proximate
> cause of his injury.[8]

Because the court found that neither party was negligent in performing
the criminal act, violation of the criminal fornication statute was held
not to be a basis for barring the plaintiff's recovery.

Finally, the court observed that "[i]n accordance with the public
policy of this state to reduce the incidence of venereal diseases, the injury
[the plaintiff] allegedly suffered is one for which he should be compensated if the case can be properly proved.... The tortious nature of [the
defendant's] conduct, coupled with the interest of this state in the prevention and control of contagious and dangerous diseases, brings [the plaintiff's] injury within [the sphere of compensable physical injury]."[9]

In another case captioned *B.N. v. K.K.,*[10] the plaintiff was
employed as a nurse in a hospital in Baltimore. The defendant was a
physician at the same hospital. For a period of several months, the plaintiff and defendant "were involved in an intimate boyfriend-girlfriend
relationship and 'engaged in acts of sexual intercourse.'"[11] During the
course of their relationship, the defendant knew he had genital herpes,
but never disclosed that fact to the plaintiff. The plaintiff was eventually
infected with genital herpes as a result of her sexual contact with the
defendant. The plaintiff sued the defendant for her injuries, charging
him with negligence, fraud, the intentional infliction of emotional
distress, and assault and battery.[12]

With respect to the plaintiff's claim that the defendant acted negligently in transmitting herpes to her, the court, after noting the traditional
elements of a claim for negligence, observed that "a [legal] duty is readily
found if it appears highly likely that the conduct in question should have
brought about the harm."[13] The court then explained that "[o]ne who
knows he or she has a highly infectious disease can readily foresee the
danger that the disease may be communicated to others with whom the
infected person comes into contact. As a consequence, the infected person
has a duty to take reasonable precautions — whether by warning others or
by avoiding contact with them — to avoid transmitting the disease."[14] In
this case, the court found that the defendant "had a duty either to refrain
from sexual contact with the plaintiff or to warn her of his condition."[15]
His failure to do so constituted a negligent breach of his duty to the plaintiff which could result in his financial liability to the plaintiff.

Finally, the Alabama Supreme Court, in a recent decision, decided that a woman who claimed that her former boyfriend negligently transmitted herpes to her may have a meritorious legal action. The court found that a trial should be held to determine the adequacy of the woman's proof.[16]

In short, it appears that the emerging trend in the legal system is to find that an individual may be found negligent if he or she fails to advise his or her partner of the risk of contracting a sexual disease. A finding of negligence may translate into a substantial financial recovery for the injured party.

Fraud — Deceit — Intentional Misrepresentation

QUESTION: What are the traditional elements of a legal cause of action based on an individual's fraud, deceit or intentional misrepresentation?

ANSWER: Generally, a claim seeking compensation for another party's fraud, deceit or intentional misrepresentation must establish:

1. that the defendant made *a false representation* to the plaintiff;
2. that the defendant *knows that her representation is false* (or believes it to be false);
3. that the defendant makes the false representation *in order to induce the plaintiff* to act (or not act) in a particular manner;
4. that the *plaintiff justifiably relies* upon the defendant's false representation in acting (or not acting); and
5. that *the plaintiff is damaged* as a result of relying on the defendant's false representation.[17]

A party's deceitful representations, which resulted in the transmission of a sexual disease to an innocent party, proved to be the basis for the imposition of liability in the leading case of *Kathleen K. v. Robert B.*[18] In this case, the plaintiff sought damages against the defendant because she contracted genital herpes allegedly by way of sexual intercourse with the defendant. The complaint sought recovery based on charges of negligence, battery, intentional infliction of emotional distress and fraud. With respect to the claim for fraud, the plaintiff charged that the defendant "deliberately misrepresented to appellant that he was free from venereal disease, and that [plaintiff], relying on such representation, had sexual intercourse with [the defendant], which she would not have done had she known the true state of affairs."[19]

The defendant urged the court to reject the plaintiff's claims on the ground that "it is not the business of courts to 'supervise the promises made between two consenting adults as to the circumstances surrounding their private sexual conduct.'"[20] The defendant requested that the court refrain from judging his responsibility to the plaintiff on the grounds that courts are obligated to recognize the right of privacy in matters relating to marriage, family and sex.[21]

The court, acknowledging the importance of the right of privacy, indicated that governmental intrusion into such matters should not be unwarranted. It explained, however, that "the right of privacy is not absolute, and in some cases, is subordinate to the state's fundamental right to enact laws which promote public health, welfare and safety, even though some laws may invade the offender's right of privacy."[22] The court determined that such was the type of conduct which plaintiff sought damages for in this action. The court explained that the plaintiff "has alleged that she sustained physical injury due to [the defendant's] tortious conduct in either negligently or deliberately failing to inform her that he was infected with venereal disease. The disease which [the plaintiff] contracted is serious and (thus far) incurable. The tortious nature of [the defendant's] conduct, coupled with the interest of this state in the prevention and control of contagious and dangerous diseases, bring [the plaintiff's] injury within the type of physical injury "for which recovery may be permitted."[23]

In the case of *B.N. v. K.K.,* which is discussed above, the plaintiff, among other claims, also charged the defendant with fraud for his transmission of genital herpes to her. With respect to this claim, the court noted that although claims of deceit, fraud and intentional misrepresentation are typically applied in a business setting, such claims may also be used in situations like this for which there may be liability for physical harm.[24] The court noted that the facts of *Kathleen K.* were very close to the facts of this case except that the defendant in this case concealed the existence of genital herpes rather than asserting that he was free of the disease. The defendant sought to establish his defense to the plaintiff's claim by indicating that he made no affirmative representation as to his good health and that he was under no duty to speak "since there was no marital or other confidential relationship between the parties."[25] The court acknowledged that "concealment cannot be the basis of an action in deceit if there is no duty to speak."[26] The question then became whether the defendant had such a duty to speak. In response to this question, the court noted that it had "recognized that if the likelihood of physical harm is present, certain tort duties may arise under the circumstances in which they otherwise would not."[27] In this case, the defendant had a general duty to disclose his condition to the plaintiff before engaging in intercourse with her. The court explained that "whether the relationship between [the plaintiff] and [the defendant] was 'confidential' in the eyes of the law or whether it was not, it was a relationship which had to make [the defendant] aware that to engage in sexual intercourse with [the plaintiff] without disclosing his condition would be highly likely to produce severe harm to a readily and clearly identifiable person."[28] Accordingly, the court held that the plaintiff had indeed stated a cause of action for fraud that was recognized in the state of Maryland.[29]

> QUESTION: Have courts elsewhere recognized a distinction between an affirmative misrepresentation and simply "saying nothing"?
> ANSWER: Yes, although many courts recognize that silence may also constitute deceit in some circumstances.

One of the traditional elements of a claim alleging deceit requires a responsible party to "make a false representation." This requirement raises the question of whether liability attaches when no misrepresentation of an individual's contagious condition is actually made by the transmitting party, but, instead, the transmitting party is merely silent as to his or her condition.

Traditionally, such silence would not constitute actionable deceit. The modern trend, however, is to fashion exceptions to this rule in order to hold the deceptive party responsible for the injury caused by his or her deceit. For example, in cases where a confidential or fiduciary relationship exists between the parties, courts have found an affirmative duty to disclose information.[30] A failure to disclose such information which results in injury to another person is often actionable. This exception, which has been found to impose a duty to affirmatively disclose information to "old friends," would seem to require disclosure by intimate sexual partners of their sexual diseases, whether they are married, engaged, or merely spending the night together.[31] This was the result reached in *B.N. v. K.K.*

The "duty to speak" requirement was recently addressed by a New York appellate court in the case of *Maharam v. Maharam*.[32] In this case, a woman commenced a suit for divorce and charged her husband with fraudulently or negligently infecting her with genital herpes.[33] The woman alleged that her husband had contacted herpes through sexual relations with other women.[34]

The New York appellate court, agreeing with the trial court, found that the woman had asserted an appropriate claim against her husband for the wrongful transmission of genital herpes under theories of either negligence or fraud. With respect to the husband's "duty to speak," the court explained:

> the thirty-one year marital relationship gave rise to an affirmative "legal duty to speak," and the allegation that the husband failed to disclose his condition adequately states a cause of action for constructive, if not actual, fraud. A duty to speak in the circumstances, given the relationship of trust between the parties, can also be predicated upon Section 2307 of the [New York] Public Health Law, which states:
>
>> Any person who, knowing himself or herself to be infected with an infectious venereal disease, and has sexual intercourse with another, shall be guilty of a misdemeanor.[35]

As the number of wrongful transmission of sexual disease cases increases, we may expect to see deceit alleged more and more frequently as a ground for recovery and, hopefully, courts imposing a "duty to speak" on the individual with a contagious sexual disease.

Assault and Battery

QUESTION: What are the traditional elements of a legal cause of action based on an individual's assault?

ANSWER: An assault is generally recognized as the act of placing the victim in fear of an imminent physical contact. Actions for assault are designed to protect individuals from fright, humiliation, and other mental disturbances.[36]

QUESTION: What are the traditional elements of a legal cause of action based on an individual's "battery"?

ANSWER: Battery is generally recognized as an offensive or harmful contact to a person resulting from an act intended to cause such contact.[37]

QUESTION: Can a person be held responsible for assault and battery by inflicting a sexually transmittable disease on another?

ANSWER: Many cases recognize that a person may be held responsible for assault and battery by wrongfully transmitting a sexual disease.

An action for assault and battery, based on the transmission of a sexual disease, was the subject of *State v. Lankford.*[38] In this early case, a Delaware court considered a claim brought by a woman against her husband for the wrongful transmission to her of syphilis. In finding that the husband's transmission of this disease to his wife constituted assault and battery, the court explained:

> A husband may commit an assault and battery upon his wife, notwithstanding the marriage relation. (citation)

> A wife in confiding her person to her husband *does not consent to cruel treatment, or to infection with a loathsome disease.* A husband, therefore, knowing that he has such a disease, and concealing the fact from his wife, by accepting her consent, and communicating the infection to her, inflicts on her physical abuse, and injury, resulting in great bodily harm; and he becomes notwithstanding his marital rights, guilty of an assault, and indeed, a completed battery. (citation)

> *If the accused knew he was infected with syphilis,* and . . . knowing that he was infected with a venereal disease, and, without informing his wife of the fact, had sexual intercourse with her after such knowledge had been communicated to him, and thereby infected her with the disease, *the jury's verdict should be guilty.*

> If the jury should find that *the accused,* during the period he had sexual relations with his wife, *did not know that he was infected with a venereal disease,* and that he did not communicate with his wife after being informed that he was infected, *their verdict should be not guilty.*[39]

In this case, the verdict was guilty.

Intentional Infliction of Emotional Distress

QUESTION: What are the traditional elements of a legal cause of action based on a party's "intentional infliction of emotional distress"?

ANSWER: The intentional infliction of emotional distress is generally recognized as (1) extreme and outrageous conduct by a party which (2) intentionally or recklessly (3) causes *severe* emotional distress and to another.[40]

In addition to the obvious physical effects caused by sexually transmitted diseases, there is usually a psychological effect felt as well by the victims. Indeed, it is not unusual for victims to become deeply depressed, rage at the individual responsible for transmitting the disease (and the opposite sex in general), and develop a "leper effect" — feeling that they are damaged goods.[41]

Recognition of the emotional distress caused by contracting a sexually transmitted disease is now being recognized by the courts in their consideration of claims for money damages based on the transmitting party's intentional infliction of emotional distress.

As noted above, the plaintiff in *B.N. v. K.K.* brought a variety of claims against the defendant for his transmission of genital herpes to her. With respect to the plaintiff's claims in this case that the defendant's conduct constituted the intentional infliction of emotional distress, the court noted that even if the defendant "did not actually intend to inflict severe emotional distress, it is enough if 'he knew' that such distress [was] certain or substantially certain, to result from his conduct; or where [he acted] recklessly in deliberate disregard of a high degree of probability that the emotional distress [would] follow."[42] The court observed that the defendant knew the nature of the disease, its painful nature and its incurability, and also that his disease was active at the time he had sex with the plaintiff. The court also observed that "the transmission of genital herpes is substantially certain to produce severe emotional distress."[43] Accordingly, the court determined that "[o]ne who knowingly engaged in conduct that is highly likely to infect another with an incurable disease of this nature, and who also is aware of the nature of the disease, not only engages in intentional or reckless conduct ... he or she has committed extreme and outrageous conduct."[44]

The court then indicated that if the plaintiff could establish the severity of her emotional distress (evidence of which was not then before the court) then she would be entitled to recover for the defendant's intentional infliction of emotional distress upon her.[45]

Increasingly, courts seem prepared to hold an individual responsible, who acts with reckless disregard of the emotional (and physical) harm which may be caused by a sexually transmitted disease and infects another.[46]

Defenses to Claims

QUESTION: Do courts recognize any defense(s) to a claim which is based on the wrongful transmission of a sexual disease?

ANSWER: It is possible for the transmitting party to assert one or more such defenses in response to such a claim. The

court deciding the matter would then have to decide
whether the claim or the defense has legal merit.

QUESTION: What legal defenses may be raised in response to a claim
             based on the wrongful transmission of a sexual disease?
ANSWER: Although this area of law continues to develop, several
             possible defenses which may be asserted by a party
             charged with wrongfully transmitting a sexual disease
             include (a) consent; (b) assumption of risk; (c) con-
             tributory or comparative negligence; (d) illegality; and
             (e) interspousal immunity. These different defenses are
             discussed below.

Consent

QUESTION: What are the traditional elements of the legal defense
             of "consent"?
ANSWER: The defense of consent is based on the long-established
             principle known as "volenti non fit injuria" — "to one
             who is willing, no wrong is done."[47] An important as-
             pect of the consent defense is that the injured party's
             consent is knowingly and willingly given.[48]

QUESTION: Doesn't a party's consent to sexual intercourse constitute
             that party's similar consent to exposure of a sexually
             transmittable disease?
ANSWER: Although some courts have held that a party's consent
             to the act of sexual intercourse constitutes a consent to
             exposure of a sexually transmittable disease, the better
             reasoned cases hold that the consent is vitiated or
             destroyed when it is procured by fraud or concealment.
             In such cases, a party's consent to sexual intercourse
             does not equate to consent to exposure of a sexually
             transmittable disease.

In an early case captioned *Deeds v. Strode,*[49] the plaintiff, in a suit
for divorce, alleged that during the time she was married (or believed she
was married) to the defendant, the defendant "without her knowledge,
connivance, privity or consent, became afflicted with a loathsome and
infectious disease, commonly and generally known as gonorrhea, and
communicated said disease to plaintiff and infected her therewith."[50]
The Idaho Supreme Court upheld the trial court's dismissal of plaintiff's
claim that the defendant was liable for deceit for the transmission of
gonorrhea to her. The court, reasoning that plaintiff's consent to the act

of sexual intercourse constituted a consent to exposure to the sexual disease, explained simply that "[i]t does not appear that the defendant in any way misled the plaintiff, that he made any false representations to her, or practiced any fraud upon her, to induce her to enter the marriage relation with him."[51] Finding the plaintiff consented to the marriage, the court determined that no recovery could be had by the plaintiff for the defendant's transmission of gonorrhea to her.[52]

The better reasoned law provides that consent to intercourse is *not* consent to infection with a sexually transmittable disease. The authoritative *Restatement (2nd) of Torts,* for example, offers the following hypothetical example:

> A consents to sexual intercourse with B, who knows that A is ignorant of the fact that B has a venereal disease. B is subject to liability to A for battery.[53]

In an important English case captioned *Regina v. Bennett,*[54] the defendant was charged with causing his thirteen-year-old niece to become intoxicated and then having sexual relations with her. The defendant was found guilty of assault because he had given his niece a venereal disease. In rejecting the proposition that the girl's consent to intercourse constituted a consent to transmission of the venereal disease, the English court explained that "[a]n assault is within the rule that fraud vitiates consent, and therefore, if the prisoner, knowing that he had a foul disease, induced his niece to sleep with him, intending to possess her, and infect her, she being ignorant of his condition, any consent which she may have given, would be vitiated, and the prisoner would be guilty of an indecent assault."[55]

Recent decisions suggest that courts are now more inclined to find that a party's consent to sexual intercourse is vitiated or extinguished by his or her partner's fraudulent concealment of the risk of infection with venereal disease. This is the result reached in the *Kathleen K.* decision, discussed above.

Assumption of Risk

QUESTION: What are the traditional elements of the legal defense of assumption of risk?

ANSWER: The defense of assumption of risk is generally established by a defendant who can show that a plaintiff's

> injury was caused by a hazard which the plaintiff was
> aware of, but who proceeded, freely and voluntarily, to
> engage in the hazardous activity nevertheless.[56]

No case has been located that considers the defense of "assumption of risk" in the context of a claim involving a sexually transmitted disease. It may be anticipated that such a defense will arise—and may even prevail—in situations where the party contracting a disease knew of the risk yet proceeded to engage in sexual activity in spite of such risk. The following section offers an analogous example.

Contributory or Comparative Negligence

QUESTION: What, traditionally, is the basis for the legal defense of contributory negligence?

ANSWER: Contributory negligence is generally established by showing that a party's own conduct is below an acceptably safe standard—which contributes to the injury he has suffered as a result of another's conduct.[57] A finding that an injured party was contributorily negligent may bar any recovery in a legal proceeding against the other individual causing injury.

QUESTION: What, traditionally, is the basis for the legal defense of comparative negligence?

ANSWER: The doctrine of comparative negligence recognizes that an injured party may be responsible, to some degree, for his injuries. Unlike contributory negligence, the degree of his responsibility will reduce proportionately—but will not bar—a claim seeking to establish the defendant's liability.[58]

An example of a lawsuit that invoked the defense of comparative negligence is the case of *Doe v. Gazzana*.[59] In this case, the plaintiff became infected with genital herpes after having sex with the defendant, whom she was dating. She thereafter brought suit alleging that the defendant negligently transmitted the disease to her. The plaintiff testified that she had noticed what she suspected was a herpes lesion before having intercourse with the defendant. A jury determined that the defendant negligently transmitted herpes to the plaintiff but found that the plaintiff was 49 percent at fault for the transmission (the defendant being 51 percent at fault). The jury awarded plaintiff $28,000 for past and future pain and suffering.

Illegality

QUESTION: What is the defense of illegality based on?

ANSWER: A number of states have enacted legislation which makes certain types of sexual activity unlawful—such as, for example, sodomy (generally oral and/or anal sex), adultery (sexual intercourse involving a married person with one other than a spouse) and fornication (generally, sexual intercourse between two unmarried persons). A defense based on illegality seeks to establish that an individual cannot recover in a court of law for injuries which result from an illegal act to which he or she was a party.

QUESTION: Will sexual intercourse between unmarried couples in states which make such an act illegal bar an individual's claim against another for the wrongful transmission of a sexual disease?

ANSWER: Possibly.

The defense of illegality may very well continue to bar an individual who contracts a sexual disease from recovering monetary damages against his or her partner in some parts of the country. In January 1990, the Virginia Supreme Court upheld the dismissal of a lawsuit in which a woman accused her former husband of giving her herpes prior to their marriage. The woman, who sought $2.5 million in damages, claimed that the transmission of herpes constituted battery, the intentional infliction of emotional distress, and negligence. The Virginia Supreme Court barred the woman from pursuing her claim because, as the court explained, "a participant in the unlawful act of fornication is barred from recovering damages resulting from that act."[60]

Interspousal Immunity

QUESTION: What is the doctrine of interspousal immunity?

ANSWER: This doctrine generally precludes one spouse from suing the other spouse for personal injuries. The doctrine was originally based on the notion that a husband and wife were "one person in law" and so could not injure the "other"—there being no "other."[61]

QUESTION: What is the current status of the interspousal immunity doctrine?

ANSWER: Many jurisdictions have eliminated the doctrine of in-
           terspousal immunity. Some jurisdictions which have
           retained this doctrine have created broad exceptions
           which provide that the intentional infliction of injury on
           a spouse, such as by assault, deceit, or intentional inflic-
           tion of emotional distress, are not protected under this
           doctrine.

Over the years, the doctrine of interspousal immunity has been
eroded. The authoritative *Restatement (Second) of Torts* now provides
that "[a] husband or wife is not immune from tort liability to the other
solely by reason of the [marital] relationship."[62] This erosion is making
it easier for a spouse to sue the other spouse for the transmission of a
sexual disease.

In *Crowell v. Crowell,*[63] a wife brought an action against her husband as a result of her having contracted a venereal disease during the
course of their marriage. The wife argued that her husband "took advantage of his marital relationship with [the] plaintiff and infected her with
[a venereal disease]."[64] The defendant simply argued that because the
parties were husband and wife at all times during the act complained of,
the plaintiff's claims should be dismissed.

The court, in considering the defendant's claim for interspousal immunity, noted that the original reason for the defense was that, upon the
parties' marriage, the wife became the husband's property. The court
then noted, in a passage worth quoting at length, that

> The origin of such treatment was perhaps natural in the economic con-
> ditions of the barbarous age when superior physical force made the
> wife the slave of the husband. But those conditions have passed. All
> the conditions and customs of life have changed. Many laws have be-
> come obsolete, even when not changed by statute and the constitution
> . . . and *no principle of justice can maintain the proposition in law, or
> in morals, that a debauchee, as the defendant admits himself to be, can
> marry a virtuous girl, and, continuing his round of dissipation, keep
> up his intercourse with lewd women, contracting, as he admits, vene-
> real disease, communicate it to his wife, as the jury finds, subjecting
> her to humiliation, and ruining her physically for life, and seeking to
> run off with all his property, abandoning her to other indigents; yet be
> exempted from all liability by the assertion that he and his wife are one,*
> and he being that one, he owes no duty to her of making reparation
> to her for the gross wrong which he has done to her.[65]

Finally, as noted above, a Delaware court, in the case of *State v.
Lankford,*[66] considered whether a husband could criminally assault and

batter his wife by giving her a venereal disease during the course of their marriage. The Delaware court found the husband chargeable with assault and battery for his wrongful transmission of syphilis to his wife.

Liability of Health Care Providers for Failure to Warn — A Footnote

With so many individuals infected with herpes, AIDS, or another contagious sexual disease, it is becoming more and more common for health-care providers, such as doctors and psychologists, to learn of their patient's infection with this disease. When this occurs, questions arise concerning the obligation, if any, which these health care professionals have to notify third parties who are at risk of contracting these diseases from their patients. When these health-care providers fail to warn third parties who later become infected, additional questions arise as to these health care providers' liability, if any, for their failure to notify these third parties. This section considers some of the developing legal responses to these questions which arise in this context.

> QUESTION: Have doctors been legally required to advise people at risk of contracting infection in cases involving communicable disease?
>
> ANSWER: In certain circumstances, doctors may be required to notify individuals at risk of contracting communicable disease.

Case law has long recognized a physician's obligation, under certain circumstances, to report about a patient's communicable disease.

For example, in *Hoffman v. Blackmon,*[67] a Florida court considered a claim brought against a physician for negligently failing to diagnose a patient's condition as tuberculosis. As a result of his failure to make the proper diagnosis, the patient's two-year-old daughter contracted the disease from her.[68] The defendant, who conceded negligence with respect to the father, argued that she owed no duty to the child, so that no liability could be established. The Florida court, disagreeing with this position, stated:

> It is recognized that once a contagious disease is known to exist, a duty arises on the part of the physician to use reasonable care to advise and warn family members of the patient's immediate family of the existence and dangers of the disease.[69]

In this case, the Florida court found the physician negligent for failing to take precautionary steps to protect the child from contracting the disease.[70]

This decision suggests that a physician treating a married individual for a contagious sexually transmissible disease may have a duty to warn the nonpatient spouse who is at risk. No case supporting this proposition, however, has been found.

> QUESTION: How have courts treated a doctor's requirement to hold his patients' information in confidence?
>
> ANSWER: Courts have adopted a balancing approach which considers not only the importance of the patient's confidentiality but also the interest in protecting innocent people from exposure to danger, including the exposure to a communicable disease.

One of the leading judicial decisions that concerns the balance between a patient's confidence and the interest of protecting innocent third parties is the case of *Tarasoff v. Regents of the University of California.*[71] In this case Prosenjit Poddar killed Tatiana Tarasoff. Tarasoff's parents alleged that Poddar had previously confided his intention to kill Tatiana to a psychologist employed by the defendant university.[72] No warning was ever given to Tatiana.[73] In finding that the treating psychologist in this case had a duty to warn Tatiana that she was at risk, the California Supreme Court explained:

> We realize that the open and confidential character of psychotherapeutic dialogue encourages patients to express threats of violence, few of which are ever executed. Certainly a therapist should not be encouraged routinely to reveal such threats; such disclosures could seriously disrupt the patient's relationship with his therapist and with the persons threatened. To the contrary, *the therapist's obligations to his patient requires that he not disclose a confidence unless such disclosure is necessary to avert danger to others, and even then that he do so discreetly,* and in a fashion that would preserve the privacy of his patient to the fullest extent compatible with the prevention of the threatened danger.[74]

The court then explained that such disclosure would *not* constitute a breach of professional ethics, stating:

> The revelation of a communication under the above circumstances is not a breach of trust or a violation of professional ethics; as stated in

the Principles of Medical Ethics of the American Medical Association (1957), section 9: "A physican may not reveal the confidence entrusted to him in the course of medical attendance . . . *unless he is required to do so by law or unless it becomes necessary in order to protect the welfare of the individual or of the community.*" We conclude that the public policy favoring protection of the confidential character of patient-psychotherapist communications *must yield to the extent to which disclosure is essential to avert danger to others. The protective privilege ends where the public peril begins.*

Our current crowded and computerized society compels the interdependence of its members. In this risk-infested society we can hardly tolerate the further exposure to danger that would result from a concealed knowledge of the therapist that his patient was lethal. If the exercise of reasonable care to protect the threatened victim requires the therapist to warn the endangered party or those who can reasonably be expected to notify him, we see no sufficient societal interest that would protect and justify concealment.[75]

The issue of balancing a patient's confidence against the right of innocent third parties has also been specifically addressed in the context of a patient's contagious disease. In the case of *Simonsen v. Swenson,*[76] the plaintiff, while working in a strange town, became afflicted with sores on his body. He went to the defendant, a physician, who diagnosed the plaintiff's sores as syphilis. The defendant then advised plaintiff to leave the hotel where he was staying so as not to communicate the disease to anyone there. When the plaintiff did not leave, the defendant advised the hotel management, who consequently forced the plaintiff to leave. The plaintiff then brought a lawsuit against the defendant for breach of a confidential relationship.[77]

The Nebraska Supreme Court, in finding that the defendant physician acted reasonably and in good faith in disclosing the plaintiff's contagious disease to the hotel, acknowledged that

The relation of physician and patient is necessarily a highly confidential one. It is often necessary for the patient to give information about himself which would be most embarrassing or harmful to him if given general circulation. This information the physician is bound, not only upon his own professional honor and the ethics of his high profession, to keep secret, but by reason of the affirmative mandate of the statute itself. A wrongful breach of such confidence, and a betrayal of such trust, would give rise to a civil action for the damages naturally flowing from such wrong. Is such a rule of secrecy then, subject to any qualifications or exceptions? The doctor's duty does not necessarily end with the patient, for on the other hand, the malady of his patient may be such that a duty may be owing to the public and, in some cases, to other particular individuals.[78]

The court justified the physician's disclosure of a patient's contagious disease to third parties at risk of exposure for the following reason:

> No patient can expect that if his malady is found to be of a dangerously contagious nature he can still require it to be kept secret from those to whom, if there was no disclosure, such disease would be transmitted. *The information given to a physician by his patient, though confidential, must, it seems to us, be given and received subject to the qualification that if the patient's disease is found to be of a dangerous and so highly contagious or infectious a nature that it will necessarily be transmitted to others unless the danger of contagion is disclosed to them, then the physician should, in that event, if no other means of protection is possible, be privileged to make so much of a disclosure to such persons as is necessary to prevent the spread of the disease.* A disclosure in such case would, it follows, not be a betrayal of the confidence of the patient, since the patient must know, when he imparts the information or subjects himself to the examination, that, in the exception stated, his disease may be disclosed.[79]

Finally, it is noted that the American Medical Association has filed the following position with respect to physicians' duty to warn:

> In the realm of duty to warn, the Council on Judicial and Ethical Affairs has outlined a course of action to be taken by physicians: Where there is no statute that mandates or prohibits reporting of seropositive individuals to public health authorities and it is clear that the seropositive individual is endangering an identified third party, the physician should (1) attempt to persuade the infected individual to cease endangering the third party; (2) if persuasion fails, notify authorities; and (3) if authorities take no action, notify and counsel the endangered third party.[80]

QUESTION: Are health-care providers required to report AIDS cases?
ANSWER: It appears that all states currently require the reporting of cases of AIDS.[81] Only a few states, however, currently require the reporting of HIV infection.[82]

Transmission of AIDS in the Course of Medical Treatment — A Footnote

It is now well known that in addition to transmission through sexual contact, AIDS can be transmitted in the course of medical treatment.

Frequently, such transmissions occur as a result of blood transfusions of HIV infected blood. Although it is now possible for blood banks to screen for the HIV virus in donated blood, individuals who received transfusions before HIV testing was available may develop (or transmit) AIDS over the years. It is also possible for health-care workers to be infected by the HIV virus in the course of performing their jobs. Although it is beyond the scope of this book to consider claims for liability arising out of such nonsexual transmissions, I note that individuals who contract AIDS under such circumstances may be entitled to recover damages for their injuries. For example, it is reported that a Denver jury awarded $5.5 million in damages to a woman and her husband after the woman contracted AIDS from blood infused during surgery which had been supplied by the defendant, a blood bank.[83] Readers interested in additional information on this subject are advised to see an attorney.

Chapter IV

Sex-based Employment Discrimination and Sexual Harassment in the Workplace

Sex-based Discrimination

Introduction

Although once unusual, it is now commonplace for women in the United States to enter the paid labor force. The entry of women into the workforce has, in many respects, resulted in a "sexual division of labor" within the United States. Many women have taken different jobs than men and, generally, are paid less for those jobs. Sometimes these wage differences are justifiable and based on legitimate employment-related criteria; sometimes they are not, and, instead, are based solely on an employee's sex. In order to address the inequity resulting from sex-based employment discrimination, various state and federal legislation has been enacted. The most significant of these laws and their impact are the subject of this section.

Title VII of the 1964 Civil Rights Act

QUESTION: What is Title VII of the Civil Rights Act of 1964?
ANSWER: A federal statute which broadly prohibits employment practices that discriminate against individuals "because of race, color, religion, sex, or national origin."[1]

82

Title VII's General Prohibition

Title VII provides that it shall be an unlawful employment practice for certain designated employers "(1) to fail or refuse to hire or to discharge any individual or otherwise to discriminate against any individual with respect to his compensation, terms, conditions or privileges of employment . . . because of such individual's race, color, religion, sex, or national origin. . . ."[2] Title VII further provides that "it shall be an unlawful employment practice for an employer. . . . (2) to limit, segregate or classify his employees or applicants for employment in any way which would deprive or tend to deprive any individual of employment opportunities or otherwise adversely affect his status as an employee, because of such individual's race, color, religion, sex or national origin."[3]

Employers Subject to Title VII

Generally, Title VII provides that employers are subject to the prohibitions of this act if they are engaged in an industry "affecting commerce" and have fifteen or more employees for each working day in each of twenty or more calendar weeks in the current or preceding calendar year.[4] Exceptions to coverage under this act include corporations wholly owned by the United States government and tax exempt private membership clubs.

Employees Protected by Title VII

Whether an individual employee is protected against unlawful discrimination under Title VII depends on whether he or she works (or is applying for work) for an employer subject to Title VII. Accordingly, independent contractors are not protected by Title VII. Title VII was extended to cover federal employees in 1972.[5]

Elements of a Title VII Case

There are four typical issues which arise in a sex discrimination case brought pursuant to Title VII. These issues are

1. *the employee's proof* of a prima facie (apparent) case of sex discrimination;
2. *the employer's defense* that the employee's claim lacks merit;
3. the employee's *opportunity to rebut* the employer's defense; and

4. the employer's opportunity to establish that a discriminatory practice is justified as a *business necessity or bona fide occupational qualification* ("BFOQ").

These various aspects of a typical Title VII claim are discussed below.

An Employee's Claim

QUESTION: What must an individual allege in a sex discrimination case brought under Title VII?

ANSWER: In order to establish a prima facie case of discrimination, an employee must allege that she has either been (1) treated less favorably than other employees because of her sex (disparate treatment) or (2) that an employer's policies have a discriminatory impact on women (disparate impact).

Disparate Treatment

An individual who believes that her employer intentionally "treats [her] less favorably than others because of [her] . . . sex . . ."[6] may be able to establish such employer's violation of Title VII for "disparately treating" its employees on the basis of sex. Essentially, disparate treatment is based on an unlawful intent to discriminate on the basis of sex (and other protected classes of workers). "Direct" proof of such an impermissible intention is often difficult to establish. It is possible, however, that such proof may be established by "circumstantial evidence."[7] For example, if a woman applies for a job she is qualified to perform, is rejected, and the job goes unfilled, she probably would establish a prima facie (apparent) disparate treatment claim. As discussed below, the defendant employer would then be given an opportunity to establish an absence of an intention to discriminate.

A review of two important case decisions helps clarify the legal aspects of a sex-based disparate treatment case.

Disparate Treatment Established

In *Armstrong v. Index Journal Co.,*[8] the plaintiff charged her employer, a daily newspaper, with violating Title VII by improperly engaging in sex-based employment discrimination. The plaintiff alleged that, because of her sex, she was assigned to a separate classification in the defendant's advertising department, called "special salesmen."[9]

Plaintiff further alleged that this classification received a lower base pay and less desirable advertising accounts than the "regular salesmen" positions, which were held exclusively by men.[10] Finally, the plaintiff alleged that as a result of her complaining about the discriminatory treatment she received, she was improperly discharged.[11]

The federal court of appeals that considered this case found that the defendant had previously advertised for the plaintiff's position in a help-wanted ad which indicated an "opening for [a] lady in advertising department."[12] The court also found that no man had ever been hired for this job. Moreover, the defendant advertised for its "regular salesmen" through male help-wanted ads and only men had held the position of "regular salesmen" at the time of trial.[13]

Although the plaintiff performed the same tasks as the male salesmen, the defendant paid her less than its male salesmen, because, it believed that the accounts that she was assigned to handle were easier accounts than those accounts which male salesmen were assigned to handle and because of the plaintiff's "lack of experience."[14]

Noting that Title VII made it an unlawful employment practice for an employer to classify his employees "for employment in any way which would deprive or tend to deprive any individual with employment opportunities ... because of such [employee's] ... sex,"[15] the court found that the record established a prima facie (i.e. apparent) case of improper sex-based disparate treatment. The court explained that the plaintiff had "demonstrated that she was a member of [a] protected class, that she was employed in a job expressly limited to the protected class and that she was excluded from a higher paid classification whose duties she [could] satisfactorily perform."[16] The court found that the defendant's segregation of jobs by sex adversely affected her status as an employee and deprived her of the opportunity to reach the maximum salary payable to salesmen.

In response to the defendant's contention that the plaintiff's qualifications were not substantially equal to that of its male salesmen, the court noted that the defendant "had no specific qualifications with respect to either education or skill and entry level positions for either female or male salesmen. The sole difference in qualifications, as demonstrated by the advertisements soliciting applicants, is that one position was reserved for women and the other for men."[17] For this reason, the court ordered the defendant to offer the plaintiff reinstatement to the advertising department at a rate of pay comparable to its male salesmen.[18]

Disparate Treatment Not Established

A review of the case of *Briggs v. City of Madison*[19] helps identify the nature of proof which an employer may present to defend against a claim of disparate treatment and establish a legitimate, nondiscriminatory reason for utilizing the challenged employment practice. In this case, plaintiffs, who were women employed as public health nurses by the defendant City of Madison, Wisconsin, Department of Public Health, alleged that the defendant discriminated against them on the basis of sex with respect to job compensation, job classification, and the terms, conditions and privileges of their employment by employing public health nurses at a lower paying classification than that of male public health sanitarians who performed jobs requiring the same or lesser degree of qualifications, skill, effort, and responsibility under similar working conditions.[20]

The court found that in order to qualify for employment as a City of Madison public health nurse, an individual must be a registered nurse, must be certified or eligible for certification as a public health nurse and must meet certain educational qualifications. The City of Madison public health nurses held a variety of duties, which they provided in public schools, private homes and health clinics. The court noted that from 1958 to 1978 all of the City of Madison public health nurses had been women, with one exception.[21]

The court then noted that the City of Madison also employed a classification of worker called "sanitarian." In order to qualify for this position, an individual must have graduated from an accredited college or university with a specialized degree. Individuals filling this position also held a variety of duties, including inspecting eating and drinking establishments, food stores, and hotels and motels in order to ensure their compliance with applicable health rules and regulations.[22] The court also found that from 1958 to 1978, all of the City of Madison's sanitarians had been men. The court noted that the city gave sanitarians a higher salary than the salary it paid to the public health nurses.[23]

In 1977, the public health nurses requested that their pay match or exceed the pay range of sanitarians. After their request was denied, they filed a complaint with the Equal Employment Opportunity Commission, alleging that the city was discriminating against the plaintiffs on the basis of sex in violation of Title VII. The lawsuit alleged that each nurse had a salary which was less than that of the sanitarian although their job qualifications were the same or greater than the job qualifications and responsibilities of sanitarians.[24]

After comparing the various duties and responsibilities of both public nurses and sanitarians, the court determined that it was reasonable to conclude that the plaintiffs had demonstrated they occupied a sex-segregated job classification that was compensated with lower wages than those paid to the occupants of the all male classification of sanitarians "in spite of the fact that the job held by the women plaintiffs required at least (possibly more) skill, effort, and responsibility than that which was required by the sanitarians in performing their jobs."[25]

In holding that the plaintiffs had established a prima facie (apparent) case of sex discrimination, the court noted that they had proved "that (1) they are members of a protected class; (2) that they occupy a sex-segregated classification; (3) that they are paid less than (4) a sex-segregated classification occupied by men; and also (5) that the two sex-segregated classifications involve work that is similar in skill, effort, and responsibility."[26]

In this case, however, the court found that evidence was offered by the city which established that in order for it to retain sanitarians, it was required to raise their salary. Evidence was submitted that a vacancy for a sanitarian position had gone unfilled for eight months and the city personnel director indicated that a sanitarian's pay scale needed to be increased in order to fill a position. The court found that the plaintiffs had *not shown* that the city's upgrading of the sanitarians pay was not a response to "a legitimate perception that pay increases were necessary in order to recruit and retain qualified sanitarians."[27] The court explained that the plaintiffs failed to produce contradictory evidence "such as the size of the labor pool from which sanitarians are recruited, or evidence of the number of applicants for each sanitarian vacancy, or the average length and time such vacancies went unfilled" to rebut the defendants' defense. In short, the plaintiffs failed to "produce the kind of hard evidence about the general availability of both sanitarians and public health nurses in the labor market during the time in question that would suffice to carry [their burden of proof]."[28] On this record, the court granted the defendants' motion to dismiss the plaintiffs' charges.

Analysis

Analysis of decided cases suggests that an employee challenging an employment practice as intentionally discriminatory, and so in violation of Title VII, has a relatively minimal burden in the first instance. For example, an individual challenging an alleged discriminatory refusal to hire practice under Title VII initially bears the burden of showing:

1. that (she) belongs to a protected class (e.g. women);
2. that (she) applied and was qualified for a job for which the employer was seeking applicants;
3. that, despite (her) qualifications, (she) was rejected; and
4. that, after (her) rejection, the position remained open and the employer continued to seek applicants from persons of (said individual's qualifications).[29]

Satisfaction of this initial "burden" by the aggrieved employee then "shifts the burden" to the employer to establish that the challenged practice is legitimate. The employer's "burden of proof" is discussed in a later section.

Disparate Impact

Title VII also prohibits the use of facially neutral employment policies which, although not necessarily adopted for the purpose of intentionally discriminating against women (or other protected classes) on the basis of their sex, do, in fact, have a "discriminatory impact" on women. An individual seeking to prove that an apparently neutral employment practice has had a disparate impact on a protected group must establish that the challenged employment practice impacts more harshly on the protected group than on others.

General Requirements

The leading Supreme Court decision on disparate impact claims is *Griggs v. Duke Power Co.*[30] In this case, the Supreme Court considered the question of whether "an employer is prohibited by [Title VII] from requiring a high school education or passing of a standardized general intelligence test as a condition of employment for a job when (a) neither standard is shown to be significantly related to successful job performance, (b) both requirements operate to disqualify Negroes at a substantially higher rate than white applicants, and (c) the jobs in question formerly had been filled only by white employees as part of a long standing practice of giving preference to whites."[31]

The Supreme Court rejected the lower court's reasoning that in considering the merits of this case, a "subjective" test of the employer's intention to discriminate (or not) should govern. In this case, the lower court found that there was no evidence that the employer held a discriminatory purpose in adopting the testing requirements. In rejecting this analysis, the Supreme Court observed that the objective of Congress in enacting Title VII "was to achieve equality of employment opportunity and remove barriers that have operated in the past to favor an identifiable group of white employees over other employees."[32] The courts have then found that "[u]nder the Act, practices, procedures, or tests neutral on their face, and even neutral in terms of intent, cannot be maintained if they operate to 'freeze' the status quo of prior discriminatory employment practices."[33]

The Supreme Court also noted that although Title VII does *not* command that an individual be hired simply because he was formerly the subject of discrimination, it *does* require the "removal of artificial, arbitrary, and unnecessary barriers to employment when the barriers operate invidiously to discriminate on the basis of racial or other impermissible classification [e.g. sexual]."[34] In short, as the Court explained, Title VII "proscribes not only overt discrimination but also practices that are *fair in form, but discriminatory in operation. The touchstone is business necessity. If an employment practice which operates to exclude Negroes cannot be shown to be related to job performance, the practice is prohibited.*"[35]

In this case, the Supreme Court found that the employer's high school completion requirement and general intelligence test did not bear a "demonstrable relationship to successful performance of the jobs for which it was used."[36] On the contrary, the Court found that both requirements were adopted without a meaningful study of their relationship to job-performance ability.[37]

As this book was being prepared, the Supreme Court handed down its decision in the case of *Wards Cove Packing Co. v. Atonio,*[38] which redefines the standards for measuring a disparate impact claim. The interested reader *must* consult this case to properly understand this very complex area of law.

Sex-based Disparate Impact Claims

Typical employment criteria that often give rise to a sex-based disparate impact claim concern height and weight requirements or physical strength requirements, as a condition for employment — when

such requirements are irrelevant to job performance. An example
of such criteria is discussed in the case of *Harless v. Duck*.[39] In this
case, a lawsuit was brought against the City of Toledo, Ohio, Police
Department by certain women who had taken a patrolman's examination which had been given in certain years.[40] This examination consisted of two written (intelligence) tests, a physical ability test, and
an oral interview. The physical ability test consisted of requiring job
applicants to complete "15 push-ups, 25 sit-ups, [a] 6-foot standing
broad jump and 25-second obstacle course."[41] This physical ability
test had a statistically significant disparate impact on female job applicants.[42]

In finding impermissible discrimination based on the glaring statistical evidence of disparate impact in this case, the court noted that there
was no justification for the types of exercises selected — or their relation
to successful job performance.[43] In addition, the police department
"had not conducted any comparison studies of the job performances of
male and female officers."[44] Accordingly, the court found it abundantly
clear that the discriminatory policies in hiring, classification, assignment, and promotion were grounded on "impermissible and archaic
traditional stereotypes."[45]

Analysis

Recognizing the difficulty inherent in proving motivation (i.e.,
motive to discriminate), courts considering Title VII claims may find
a prima facie case of discrimination by examining the impact an employment practice may have on protected groups, such as women. If a
practice has an uneven or disparate impact on these groups, the complaining individual has met the first test for establishing a Title VII
violation.

Employer Defenses

QUESTION: How can an employer defend against a case of alleged
sex discrimination brought pursuant to Title VII?

ANSWER: As demonstrated in several of the cases reviewed above,
an employer may seek to controvert, as a factual matter,
the plaintiff's case by establishing an absence of an intention to discriminate (for disparate treatment claims)

or establishing that the plaintiff's (statistical) proof in a disparate impact case is inaccurate. In addition, a narrow exception to the general rule against discrimination may allow an employer to make an employment decision which has an adverse effect on women if the employer can establish that the criteria selected which causes such an effect has an overriding legitimate business purpose or is a bona fide occupational qualification reasonably necessary to the normal operation of the employer's business.

Generally

The Supreme Court addressed an employer's defense to a Title VII claim in the case of *Furnco Construction Corp. v. Waters.*[46] In this case, the Court observed that when an employee alleges a prima facie case of employment discrimination under Title VII, by either establishing disparate treatment or disparate impact, the burden shifts to the employer to establish that the challenged employment practice was based on a legitimate consideration, and not an illegitimate one such as sex.[47] The employer may establish a legitimate basis for the decision without proving an absence of an intention to discriminate.

The court also explained that the employer "need not prove that he pursued the course which would both enable him to achieve his own business goal *and* allow him to consider the *most* employment applications. Title VII prohibits him from having as a goal a work force selected by any proscribed discriminatory practice, *but it does not impose a duty to adopt a hiring procedure that maximizes hiring of minority employees* . . . the employer need only 'articulate some legitimate, nondiscriminatory reason for the employee's rejection.'"[48]

The Supreme Court explained, however, that an employer's proof of a permissible business justification which is reasonably related to the achievement of a legitimate business goal does not necessarily end the inquiry into the merits of an employee's Title VII claim. At that point, as discussed below, the plaintiff "must be given the opportunity to introduce evidence that the proffered justification is merely a pretext for discrimination."[49]

As previously noted, the reader should consult the Supreme Court's recent decision in *Wards Cove Packing Co.* for an update on this analysis.

The Business Necessity Defense

In a case alleging either disparate treatment or the disparate impact of an employment policy, an employer may rebut the plaintiff's case by establishing that the challenged employment policy is a "business necessity."

Courts applying the test of business necessity are prone to use different standards for measuring the legitimacy of the employer's challenged conduct. Applicability of the standard also varies depending on whether the individual challenge is based on alleged disparate treatment or disparate impact.

In a disparate treatment case, the Supreme Court explained the nature of an employer's burden as follows: "[w]hen the plaintiff has proved a prima facie case of discrimination, the defendant bears only the burden of explaining clearly the nondiscriminatory reasons for its actions."[50]

An employer's burden in a disparate impact case is addressed in the *Wards Cove Packing* case.

Women's Rights v. Fetal Rights

One of the most interesting examples of the business necessity defense in a disparate impact case concerns employment decisions which exclude fertile women from certain jobs in order to protect unborn children from hazards in the workplace. The many complex issues raised in these situations cannot be fully explored in this book and the interested reader is urged to consult his or her attorney for additional information. An example of one court's handling of some of these issues is in the case of *Wright v. Olin Corp.*[51] In this case, the employer maintained a "fetal vulnerability" program which restricted female access to jobs requiring contact with toxic chemicals.[52] The program was challenged as disparately treating and impacting on women. The court recognized as the threshold question in this case as "whether under any circumstances the protection of workers' unborn children can properly be considered such a necessity."[53] The court then explained the business necessity test by noting that:

> [its] original application, in a challenge to the use of intelligence tests and diploma requirements, was to the most obviously job-related "necessity" of being able effectively to perform the job in question. Since

> *Griggs,* the necessity contemplated has been held to run as well to considerations of workplace safety. In our own frequently cited and applied formulation in *Robinson v. Lorillard Corp.,* (citation omitted), Judge Sobeloff put it that the *"test is whether there exists an overriding legitimate business purpose such that the practice is necessary to the safe and efficient operation of the business."* (emphasis added). And the Supreme Court has since also put it that the necessity runs to "safe and efficient job performance." *Dothard v. Rawlinson* (citation omitted).[54]

The court then explained that while the overriding purpose of Title VII is to allow women to make their own employment decisions, that consideration does not always apply when the safety of others is at stake.[55]

As this book was being prepared, the Supreme Court was considering the case of Auto Workers v. Johnson Controls Inc.[56] The reader should watch for this decision, as it will surely help clarify this area of law.

The "Bona Fide Occupational Qualification" Defense

In addition to the business necessity defense, Title VII also permits employers to make certain decisions based on sex if sex is a bona fide occupational qualification ("BFOQ") reasonably necessary to the normal operation of the employer's business.[57] Courts considering the applicability of a BFOQ defense typically consider whether an employer designates the particular job at issue as requiring a member of only one sex and, if so, is the requirement necessary.

BFOQ Defense Established

The BFOQ defense was considered by the Supreme Court in the case of *Dothard v. Rawlinson.*[58] In this case, the Supreme Court considered the claim of the plaintiff who unsuccessfully sought employment with the Alabama Board of Corrections as a prison guard. After her application was rejected, she brought a claim under Title VII alleging that she had been denied employment because of her sex. The plaintiff charged that she had been refused employment because she did not meet a 120 pound weight requirement which had been established by Alabama law. The plaintiff, who did not claim that the statutory height and weight requirements intentionaly discriminated against women, alleged that, in practice, these qualifications disproportionately excluded women from eligibility for employment with the Alabama Board of Corrections.[59] After noting that the plaintiff had established that these statutory height and weight standards had a discriminatory impact on women applicants, the Supreme Court considered the defendant's arguments that these requirements were job related and a business necessity.

The defendant alleged that these height and weight requirements were "job related" because a sufficient (but unspecified) amount of strength was essential to effective job performance as a correctional counselor in the Alabama prison system.[60] The Supreme Court observed, however, that the defendant "produced no evidence correlating the height and weight requirements with the requisite amount of strength thought essential to good job performance."[61] The Court explained that "if the job-related quality that the [defendants] identify as a bona fide, their purpose could be achieved by adopting and validating a test for applicants that measures strength directly. Such a test, fairly administered, would fully satisfy the standards of Title VII because it would be one that 'measure[s] the person for the job and not the person in the abstract.'"[62]

With respect to the defendant's assertion that the height and weight requirements were bona fide occupational qualifications reasonably necessary to the normal operations of the Alabama prison system, the court explained that although this exception is intended to be a narrow exception to the general prohibition against employment discrimination on the basis of sex, on the particular factual circumstances of this case, the Court found that the state's height and weight qualifications did indeed fall within the narrow contours of this exception. The Court explained that "the environment in Alabama's penitentiaries is a peculiarly inhospitable one for human beings of whatever sex."[63] It noted that in the usual case, the argument "that a particular job is too dangerous for women may appropriately be met by the rejoinder that it is the purpose of Title VII to allow the individual woman to make that choice for herself."[64]

In this case, however, more than just the individual woman's decision is at stake. The Court explained that the essence of a correctional counselor's duties is to maintain prison security. In this case, the Court found that "there is a basis in fact for expecting that sex offenders who have criminally assaulted women in the past would be moved to do so again if access to women were established within the prison. There would also be a real risk that other inmates, deprived of a normal heterosexual environment, would assault women guards because they were women. In a prison system where violence is the order of the day, where inmate access to guards is facilitated by dormitory living arrangements, where every institution is understaffed, and where a substantial portion of the inmate population is composed of sex offenders mixed at random with other prisoners, there are few visible deterents to inmate assaults on women custodians."[65]

Based on the evidence that was submitted, the Supreme Court concluded that being a male is a bona fide occupational qualification for the job of correctional counselor in the specific "context" of a position in an Alabama male maximum-security penitentiary.[66]

BFOQ Defense Not Established

Historically, airlines sought to employ only women to fill flight attendant positions because, they believed, their passengers preferred women over men. Courts have routinely rejected such purported passenger preference as constituting a BFOQ. For example, in *Diaz v. Pan Am World Airways, Inc.,*[67] a federal court explained:

> We begin with the proposition that the use of the word "necessary" in [Title VII] requires that we apply a business *necessity* test, not a business *convenience* test. That is to say, discrimination based on sex is valid only when the *essence* of the business operations would be undermined by not hiring members of one sex exclusively.[68]

The court then observed tha the primary *function* (essence) of an airline is to transport passengers. Acknowledging that while a pleasant environment, which may be enhanced by the effect that female stewardesses provide, their apparent ability to perform the duties of a flight attendant in a more effective manner than most men, while important, is, nevertheless, tangential to the essence of the business involved.[69] In other words, having male stewards will not so seriously effect the operation of an airline as to "jeopardize or even minimize its ability to provide safe transportation from one place to another...."[70] The court then explained that

> Because the non-mechanical aspects of the job of flight cabin attendant are not "reasonably necessary to the normal operation" of Pan Am's business, Pan Am cannot exclude *all* males simply because *most* males may not perform adequately....[71]

With respect to the airline's contention that the public generally preferred women flight attendants over male attendants the court held:

> We do not feel that the fact that Pan Am's passengers prefer female stewardesses should alter our judgment. On this subject, EEOC guidelines state that a BFOQ ought not be based on "the refusal to hire an individual because of the preferences of co-workers, the employer, clients or customers. . . ." 29 CFR 1604.1(iii).

> While we recognize that the public's expectation of finding one sex in a particular role may cause some initial difficulty, it would be totally anomalous if we were to allow the preferences and prejudices of the customers to determine whether the sex discrimination was valid. Indeed, it was, to a large extent, these very prejudices the Act was meant to overcome. Thus, we feel that *customer preference may be taken into account only when it is based on the company's inability to perform the primary function or service it offers.*[72]

Employee Rebuttal

QUESTION: If an employer relies on a recognized defense to an employee's Title VII claim, may the employee still win her case of illegal sex-based employment discrimination?

ANSWER: Yes.

Employee Rebuttal in a Disparate Treatment Case

In a disparate treatment case, after an employer articulates a nondiscriminatory reason for its treatment of the plaintiff-employee, the plaintiff-employee may be able to establish that the employer's defense is a "pretext" and, in fact, that the employer was actually motivated by an intent to discriminate against the plaintiff-employee. Such pretext may be proven by, among other things, establishing that the employer's defense is not believable or by establishing that a discriminatory intention is a more likely explanation for the employer's challenged action.

The Supreme Court considered an employee's opportunity to rebut a defense to a disparate treatment claim in the case of *Texas Department of Community Affairs v. Burdine.*[73] In this case, the Supreme Court explained that, after the plaintiff establishes a prima facie case of discrimination, the burden shifts to the defendant employer to rebut the presumption of discrimination by producing evidence that the plaintiff was rejected, or someone else was preferred, for a legitimate, non-discriminatory reason. If the defendant articulates a nondiscriminatory reason, the plaintiff then must be given the opportunity to demonstrate that the proffered reason was not the true reason for the employment decision but was, in fact, a mere pretext.[74]

Employee Rebuttal in a Disparate Impact Case

In a case challenging the disparate impact of an employment practice, after an employer articulates a business necessity to a challenged employment policy, an employee may still successfully prove a Title VII violation by establishing that a "less discriminatory alternative" to the challenged practice was available to the employer. The Supreme Court considered the "less discriminatory alternative" claim in the case of *Albermarle Paper Co. v. Moody.*[75] In this case, the plaintiffs brought an action for Title VII violations against the defendant employer to, among other things, enjoin the employer's testing program (which allegedly, measured nonverbal intelligence and verbal facility).[76] The tests disproportionately excluded racial minorities. Although the employer sought to validate the value of the tests through an industrial psychologist, the Supreme Court found that "discriminatory tests are impermissible unless shown, by professionally acceptable methods, to be 'predictive of or significantly correlated with important elements of work behavior which comprise or are relevant to the job or jobs for which candidates are being evaluated.'"[77]

Miscellaneous Issues

The Significance of Physical Capabilities

QUESTION: Are generally recognized physical capabilities of the sexes appropriate grounds for making employment decisions?

ANSWER: Many courts hold that an individual job applicant should have the opportunity to demonstrate her ability to perform a job the employer might otherwise believe can only be filled by a man.

In *Weeks v. Southern Bell Telephone & Telegraph Co.,*[78] a female employee sued her employer because she had been rejected from a position she sought to hold because, the employer believed, the position involved regular lifting of items weighing in excess of thirty pounds.[79] The employer believed that such performance could not be performed by women.[80] Accordingly, the employer sought to justify the "male only" requirement as a BFOQ.

In rejecting the proffered defense, the court found that the employer had not established "reasonable cause to believe ... that all or substantially all women would be unable to perform safely and efficiently the duties of the job involved."[81] The court then observed that

> *Title VII* rejects just this type of romantic paternalism as unduly Victorian and instead *vests individual women with the power to decide whether or not to take on unromantic tasks.* Men have always had the right to determine whether the incremental increase in remuneration for strenuous, dangerous, obnoxious, boring or unromantic tasks is worth the candle. *The promise of Title VII is that women are now to be on equal footing.* We cannot conclude that by including the bona fide occupational qualification exception Congress intended to renege on that promise.[82]

Customer Preference

QUESTION: Is customer preference an appropriate ground for an employer to use in selecting individuals of one sex over another sex in filling a job?

ANSWER: The Equal Employment Opportunity Commission guidelines provide that a bona fide occupational qualification should not be based on "the refusal to hire an individual because of the preference of ... clients or customers."[83] As discussed above in the case of *Diaz v. Pan American World Airways,* courts reject as improper discriminatory employment decisions based solely on customer preference.

Federal Constitutional Protection

QUESTION: Does the U.S. Constitution prohibit sex-based employment discrimination?

ANSWER: Although there are a number of requirements which frequently make constitutional protection unavailable, it is theoretically possible that an individual may be protected by the U.S. Constitution from sex-based employment discrimination. Generally, constitutional protection is afforded only to government employees because of the requirement that "state action" exist in order to give rise to protection.

Equal Protection Clause

The Fourteenth Amendment to the U.S. Constitution provides, in relevant part, that states shall not "deny to any person within its jurisdiction the equal protection of the laws. . . ."[84] Although private employers with no connection to state or federal government are not generally accountable under the Equal Protection Clause for acts of sex based discrimination in employment decisions, state government employees or employers whose business involves "state action" are subject to the provisions (and prohibitions) of the Equal Protection Clause. Although it is impractical to provide here a detailed discussion of the "state action" requirement, it is noted that it is possible that "private action" may be so permeated with state policy as to become subject to the constitutional limitations which are imposed upon states.

The Equal Protection Clause has been invoked in a wide variety of contexts. For example, in *Skadegaard v. Farrell,*[85] a female employee of a state agency sued her supervisory personnel under the Fourteenth Amendment, claiming sexual harassment and an illegal conspiracy to retaliate against her for rebuffing sexual advances. In finding that the plaintiff had properly proceeded under the Fourteenth Amendment, the court explained:

> An equal protection claim arises when an individual contends that he [or she] is receiving different treatment from that received by other individuals similarly situated." (citation) The requirement of state action under the Fourteenth Amendment is satisfied if there is "involvement of a state official ... whether or not the actions ... were officially authorized, or lawful; (citations omitted). Since plaintiff here alleges that she was intentionally treated differently from men at [her job] because of her sex by state officials, she has stated a claim for relief under the Equal Protection Clause."[86]

It is noted that some courts have held that the existence of federal statutory protection against discrimination (i.e. Title VII) acts as a bar to asserting claims directly under the Constitution.[87] It is also possible that other technical legal doctrines (such as the Doctrines of Sovereign Immunity and Legislative Immunity) may limit the availability of federal constitutional protection.

Due Process Clause

The Due Process Clause of the Fifth Amendment provides, in relevant part, that "no person shall be . . . deprived of life, liberty or property without due process of law. . . ."[88] As interpreted, the Due Process Clause protects employees of the federal government from employment-based discrimination. Like the Equal Protection Clause, the Due Process Clause has been invoked in a variety of contexts.

Protection under the Due Process Clause may be unavailable when Title VII applies and may be unavailable in instances where the Doctrines of Sovereign Immunity and Legislative Immunity apply.

Freedom of Speech

The First Amendment guarantees the freedom of speech by providing, in pertinent part, that "Congress shall make no law . . . abridging the freedom of speech. . . ."

It is possible that the safeguards of free speech may be used in some circumstances to prohibit sex based employment discrimination. For example, in a case captioned *Woerner v. Brzeczek,*[89] women police officers brought an action in federal court against the City of Chicago and its supervisors for sexual harassment sustained in the course of employment. After voicing complaints, the women suffered a series of retaliatory acts.[90] The plaintiffs alleged that the retaliatory acts violated their First Amendment right to freedom of speech (to voice their complaints).[91] The court held that the employees' complaints—which was neither disruptive nor against the public interest—may be entitled to constitutional protection.[92]

The Equal Pay Act

QUESTION: What is the Equal Pay Act?
ANSWER: The Equal Pay Act is a federal law that prohibits sex based wage discrimination for "equal work on jobs the performance of which requires equal skill, effort, and responsibility, and which are performed under similar working conditions."[93]

QUESTION: Who is subject to the Equal Pay Act?
ANSWER: The Equal Pay Act applies to employers engaged in

commerce or in the production of goods for commerce
and to all employees of enterprises engaged in interstate
commerce or the production of goods for commerce
with two or more employees so engaged with a gross
volume of business of $250,000. The Equal Pay Act
also applies to labor organizations dealing with such
employers and to state and local governments.[94]

QUESTION: How are jobs determined to be equal (or not)?
ANSWER: The critical element of job equality is job content
and responsibilities — not the job title.

In *Pearce v. Wichita County, City of Wichita Falls, Texas Hospital
Board,*[95] a federal appellate court considered the claim of a woman
employed by a hospital as a "Credit Clerk." Her starting pay was $385
per month, which had increased to $540 per month when she was
discharged.[96] After the woman was discharged (while earning $540 per
month) she was replaced by a male Credit Manager who earned a starting salary of $850 per month, which was increased to $1100 per month
only several months later.[97] Upon learning of this wage differential, the
woman brought an action against the hospital for violation of the Equal
Pay Act.

In finding a prima facie (apparent) violation of the Equal Pay Act,
the federal court explained that

A prima facie Equal Pay Act case requires a showing that the *employer
pays different wages to employees of opposite sexes 'for equal work on
jobs the performance of which requires equal skill, effort and responsibility, and which are performed under similar working conditions.'*
(citation) To establish "equal work," the employee need not prove that
the duties performed are identical, but merely that the "skill, effort and
responsibility" required in the performance of the jobs is "substantially
equal." (citation) The employees whose pay is the subject of comparison may hold jobs in succession as well as simultaneously.[98]

In this case, the court found that the comparison between the plaintiff's position and her successor's position was appropriate. Because the
plaintiff established that her salary upon termination was $310 less than
the starting salary of her replacement, and that they performed their
jobs under similar working conditions, the court found that the Equal
Pay Act had been violated. As a result the court awarded the plaintiff
money damages as compensation.

QUESTION: Does the Equal Pay Act authorize any justification for establishing a pay differential?

ANSWER: There are four circumstances which the act recognizes as permitting pay differential: (1) a seniority system; (2) a merit system; (3) a system where pay is based on the quantity or quality of an employee's production; and (4) a disparity which is not based on sex. The reader interested in learning more about these specific exceptions should consult their attorney.

State Protection

Many states have enacted their own laws prohibiting sex discrimination in employment. Many of these laws provide *broader* coverage than that provided by federal law. The interested reader should investigate this matter further with a knowledgeable source.

In addition, many states have enacted laws which prohibit, as a matter of state law, sex-based pay discrimination. These laws might also offer broader protection than that provided by federal law and merit further investigation by the interested reader.[99]

Miscellaneous Protection Against Discrimination — A Footnote

Besides the specific federal and state laws discussed above, other (less frequently used) laws might offer some additional protection against discrimination. The interested reader should investigate this matter further.

Pregnancy Discrimination

QUESTION: Are there laws that prohibit employers from maintaining policies that adversely impact on or disparately treat pregnant employees?

ANSWER: Yes.

In 1978, Congress enacted the Pregnancy Discrimination Act as part of Title VII. This Act, in relevant part, provides that women "affected by pregnancy, childbirth, or related medical conditions shall be treated the same for all employment-related purposes ... as other persons not so affected but similar in their ability or inability to work...."[100]

This act essentially provides that maternity must be treated like other temporary disabilities for purposes of sick leave and the availability of other disabilty benefits.

The EEOC has established guidelines on pregnancy discrimination which provide, in relevant part, that

> [a] written or unwritten employment policy or practice which excludes ... employment applicants or employees because of pregnancy, childbirth or related medical conditions is in prima facie violation of Title VII.[101]

QUESTION: Are unmarried employees entitled to the benefits of the Pregnancy Discriminaton Act?

ANSWER: The EEOC and some courts have taken the position that unmarried pregnant employees are entitled to the same benefits as married pregnant employees.[102]

QUESTION: May pregnant employees be compelled to take maternity leave?

ANSWER: Generally not unless an employer can establish that the pregnant employee's continued employment poses a risk of harm to herself, her fetus, or third parties.

In *Cleveland Board of Education v. LaFleur,*[103] the Supreme Court considered the claims of pregnant public school teachers who were required, by local rules, to take mandatory (unpaid) maternity leave five months before the expected childbirth.[104] The school board sought to justify their policy by contending they needed time to find replacements and maintain continuity and because some teachers become incapable of performing their duties during the later part of pregnancy.[105]

In invalidating the school board rules, the Court held that their containing an irrebuttable presumption of physical incompetency as to every woman was too broad a rule.[106]

In *Levin v. Delta Airlines, Inc.,*[107] a federal appellate court considered an airline's policy of removing pregnant flight attendants from flight duty. Evidence indicated that *not* all women were overcome by nausea and fatigue *but* those that were would be unable to perform their duties, which could jeopardize the safety of the people on board. Because it would be impossible to identify those pregnant women which might suffer, and those which would not, the airline excluded *all* pregnant attendants from flight duty. The court recognized this position as reasonable, stating:

[the airline's] commitment to safety in comparable matters ... enables the airline to justify the particular practice under the BFOQ doctrine. Thus, pregnancy is not a BFOQ with respect to all airlines as a transcendent matter of law. Rather, the determination is fact-specific, and it will be open to plaintiffs suing any particular carrier to demonstrate that the employer's purported fidelity to safety concerns as being at the essence of its operations is belied by inconsistent practices. The district court here held that [the airline's] commitment to safety was sufficient to sustain its BFOQ defense of the pregnancy policy, and that [the airline] does not permit persons with medical conditions comparable to pregnancy in their effect on safety to serve as flight attendants.[108]

QUESTION: May an employer maintain a policy of terminating an employee who becomes pregnant?

ANSWER: Such employment policies have been declared unconstitutional by several courts.

QUESTION: Are employers obligated to allow pregnant employees to take voluntary leave from employment prior to such time when the pregnant employee is physically disabled by her pregnancy or childbirth from performing her job?

ANSWER: As soon as a woman is actually disabled by her pregnancy or childbirth, she must be afforded the same benefits as any other temporarily disabled employee.[109]

QUESTION: Are employers required to provide maternity leave?

ANSWER: An employer is generally under no obligation to provide maternity leave except that if leaves of absence are permitted for other personal reasons, an employer may be required to offer maternity leaves. Some states may have laws requiring employees to provide maternity leave with a guarantee of reinstatement — regardless of whether those benefits are provided for other reasons.[110]

QUESTION: Are employers required to reinstate an employee following a pregnancy leave?

ANSWER: Such an employee should be treated the same as other employees seeking to return from voluntary or disability leave.

Sexual Harassment

Introduction

The preceding section concerned the problems some women face in seeking employment opportunities with employers which, for one reason or another, choose (or would prefer to choose) men to fill particular jobs over women. In one respect, this section considers almost the extreme opposite problem other women face in the course of their employment: their employers, supervisors, or coworkers "want them too much" — and for more than just job performance. Generally speaking, when women are faced with unwelcome sexual advances at work, they are being sexually harassed. The legal aspects of sexual harassment are explored in this section.

The Nature of Sexual Harassment—Generally

QUESTION: What conduct constitutes actionable sexual harassment in the workplace?

ANSWER: It is impossible to chronicle every type of action which may constitute illegal sexual harassment; every situation is different and the facts of each situation determines the existence (or not) of actionable sexual harassment. Some guidelines for determining the existence of sexual harassment (or not) have been provided by the Equal Employment Opportunity Commission, which has indicated that "[u]nwelcome sexual advances, requests for sexual favors, and other verbal or physical conduct of a sexual nature constitute sexual harassment when (1) submission to such conduct is made either explicitly or implicitly a term or condition of an individual's employment, (2) submission to or rejection of such conduct by an individual is used as the basis for employment decisions affecting such individual, or (3) such conduct has the purpose or effect of unreasonably interfering with an individual's work performance or creating an intimidating, hostile, or offensive working environment."[111] The Supreme Court's consideration of these guidelines is discussed below.

In 1980, sixteen years after the enactment of Title VII (which, as discussed in the preceding section, banned certain kinds of discrimination in employment), the EEOC issued guidelines, quoted in part above, which held that sexual harassment may also constitute a violation of Title VII. The EEOC's position was the subject of much disagreement and confusion in the courts and legal system until 1986. In that year, the Supreme Court, in a case captioned *Meritor v. Vinson,*[112] ruled that sexual harassment was indeed a violation of Title VII. A review of the *Vinson* decision is required in order to understand the current status of the law of sexual harassment.

The Facts

Michelle Vinson began work at a bank in 1974 as a teller-trainee. Over the next four years, she was promoted to bank teller, head teller, and assistant branch manager. Her promotions were undisputedly based solely on her merits as an employee at the bank. Vinson claimed that in May 1975, her supervisor took her to dinner and suggested that they have sexual relations. When she refused, her supervisor told Vinson that she "owed him" for his help in getting her a job at the bank. Fearful of losing her job if she did not consent, she engaged in sexual intercourse between forty to fifty times with the supervisor between May 1974 and 1977. The evidence also indicated that Vinson was fondled by the supervisor on the job, sometimes in front of coworkers, and that he exposed himself to her in the women's restroom.[113]

In September 1978, Vinson took indefinite sick leave from her job for which she was fired two months later. After the termination of her job at the bank, Vinson brought an action against her former supervisor and the bank, under Title VII, seeking compensatory and punitive damages for the sexual harassment she suffered while on the job.[114]

The Litigation

Vinson's claim was initially brought in the United States District Court for the District of Columbia.

The district court rejected Vinson's claim that she had been sexually harassed for three reasons:

1. it found that the relationship with her supervisor had been voluntary;
2. it found that Vinson's sexual relationship was unrelated to the bank's employment decisions which affected her (i.e. there was not a "quid pro quo" offered by the bank in exchange for her sexual favors); and
3. it found that because Vinson had never complained to the bank about her supervisor's conduct, the bank could not be liable for his actions because it had not received notice of his conduct (rejecting the EEOC's position that management could be held strictly liable for its employees' conduct).[115]

The U.S. Court of Appeals for the District of Columbia Circuit reversed the district court's opinion and found that the circumstances of this case constituted actionable sexual harassment.[116] On appeal to the Supreme Court, Vinson's claims were ultimately upheld. The Supreme Court's analysis of this case helps clarify the nature of a sexual harassment case.

Unwelcome Sexual Advances

The EEOC's 1980 guidelines concerning sexually harassing conduct, noted above, which includes "unwelcome sexual advances," was approved by the Supreme Court. Rejecting the district court's finding that Vinson's relationship with her supervisor had been voluntary, the Court, in discussing the significance of "unwelcomeness," held that "[t]he correct inquiry is whether [Vinson] by her conduct indicated the alleged sexual advances were unwelcome, not whether her actual participation in sexual intercourse was voluntary."[117]

In other words, the Supreme Court held that merely *consenting* to sexual intercourse does not establish that intercourse was *welcome*. To determine the welcomeness of sexual advances, the fact finder must consider the "totality of circumstances, such as the nature of the sexual advances and the context in which the alleged incidents occurred."[118]

Quid Pro Quo/Hostile Environment — Two Types of Actionable Harassment

The Supreme Court then observed that the EEOC recognized two general categories of sexual harassment which were cognizable under Title VII. These two categories are:

1. *"Quid Pro Quo"* harassment, which occurs when an employee is forced to choose between acquiescing to sexual demands or suffering adverse employment consequences, including losing her job;[119] and
2. *"Hostile Environment"* harassment, which occurs when workplace practices constituting unwelcome "verbal or physical conduct of a sexual nature" has the "purpose or effect of unreasonably interfering with an individual's work performance or creating an intimidating, hostile or offensive working environment."[120]

The Supreme Court explained that the "hostility" caused by the sexual harassment in this second category must be severe or pervasive enough to "alter the conditions of [the victim's] employment and create and abusive working environment."[121]

The *Vinson* decision confirmed that Title VII offers protection not just against economic forms of discrimination, but against factors which improperly affect the psychological aspect of the workplace environment. In *Vinson,* the Supreme Court's recognition of the "hostile environment" claim allowed the plaintiff to proceed with her claim even though her sexual relationship with her supervisor had not directly affected her job status within the bank.

Provocative Speech or Dress as Relevant Factors in Determining the Existence of Harassment

QUESTION: Is an employee's sexually provocative speech or dress relevant in determining whether that employee finds sexual advances unwelcome?

ANSWER: In *Vinson,* the Supreme Court stated that such conduct by an employee is "obviously relevant" in determining whether sexual advances are unwelcome.[122]

Freedom to Flirt?

QUESTION: Does every sexually based slur, innuendo, or flirtation rise to the level of actionable sexual harassment?

ANSWER: No.

In *Vinson,* the Supreme Court explained that in order for workplace (mis)conduct to rise to the level of sexual harassment, it must be "sufficiently severe or pervasive 'to alter the conditions of [the victim's] employment and create an abusive working environment.'"[123] Application of this standard in practice is often uncertain and there is no "litmus test" for predicting judicial results. Perhaps the reader's common sense is the best guide for helping predict how a court might respond to a claim for sexual harassment. Specific examples of these types of claims are considered below.

Employer Liability for Employee Misconduct

QUESTION: Are employers automatically liable for their employee(s)' sexual harassment of other employees?

ANSWER: No. [This question can be of tremendous importance to a prospective plaintiff from a financial perspective — employers typically have much more money (than the culpable employee) available to satisfy a judgment which a plaintiff may obtain in a lawsuit.]

In *Vinson,* the Supreme Court rejected both the (district court's) position that an employer cannot be held liable for an employee's sexual harassment unless it has notice of such conduct and (the court of appeal's) position that employers are automatically liable for their employee's conduct which results in the sexual harassment of other employees. Instead, the Supreme Court approved of the EEOC's position that courts should look to traditional agency principles to help determine whether employers are liable for their employees' misconduct. With respect to "quid pro quo" cases, the Court explained that

> Where a supervisor exercises authority actually delegated to him by his employer, by making or threatening to make decisions affecting the employment status of his subordinates, such actions are properly imputed to the employer whose delegation of authority empowered the supervisor to undertake them.[124]

This position usually results in finding an employer liable for "quid pro quo" sexual harassment committed by its employees — even in the absence of the employer's notice of such conduct.[125]

With respect to an employer's liability in "hostile environment" cases, the EEOC has taken the position that proof of an employer's liability depends upon consideration of such factors as (1) whether the employer knew or should have known of the harassment; (2) whether the culpable employee was acting within the scope of his employment; (3) and whether the employer properly (or recklessly) supervised the culpable employee.[126]

Summary

Understanding this general framework which the Supreme Court articulated in the *Vinson* decision makes it possible to more meaningfully examine specific aspects of sexual harassment claims. The following sections undertake this examination.

Quid Pro Quo Sexual Harassment

QUESTION: What type of conduct has been recognized as constituting quid pro quo sexual harassment?

ANSWER: Although every case must be examined in light of its
own particular facts and circumstances, generally, this
type of sexual harassment is recognized by a sexual advance made on an employee, followed by rejection, followed, in turn, by adverse employment consequences.

The case of *Williams v. Saxbe*[127] is one of the leading decisions
addressing the elements of a claim for quid pro quo sexual harassment.
In this case, the plaintiff charged that she had a "good working relationship with [her immediate supervisor] up until she refused a sexual
advance" made by him.[128] The supervisor, thereafter, harassed and
humiliated her by undeservedly reprimanding her, refusing to inform
her of pertinent job information, and generally refusing to recognize her
as competent.[129]

The plaintiff, who was thereafter terminated, later brought a lawsuit charging that her supervisor's sexual harassment constituted a Title
VII violation. The defendant presented an interesting defense: the plaintiff was denied employment opportunities *not because she was a woman,
but rather because she decided not to furnish "sexual consideration" for
job security and advancement.*[130] Accordingly, the defendant alleged,
plaintiff had not stated a Title VII violation because the discrimination
which she sustained was not based on gender.

The court rejected the defendant's position, noting that "the conduct of the plaintiff's supervisor created an artificial barrier to employment which was placed before one gender and not the other...."[131] In
finding that the plaintiff had properly asserted a Title VII violation, the
court observed:

> Plaintiff had alleged that subsequent to her rejection of her supervisor's
> advances as well as her supervisor's rejection of her request for a pro-
> motion, her supervisor began a program of harassment and criticism
> designed to have her employment terminated. *The inference drawn was
> that since she had refused to submit to the sexual condition of her
> supervisor, he had retaliated by creating a basis for her discharge from
> the agency.* The connection between the advances of her supervisor,
> which advances were not disputed, and the subsequent criticism by the
> supervisor of her work, was supported by the timing of the incident:
> the commencement of his criticisms of her alleged employment de-
> ficiencies when there had been no prior proof of criticism.[132]

This type of conduct is the essence of "quid pro quo" harassment.

> QUESTION: Is direct evidence of adverse employment consequences necessary to establish quid pro quo harassment?
> ANSWER: Courts are typically willing to examine the circumstantial evidence in support of a claim of harassment in order that an employer may not "sexually harass a female employee with impunity by carefully stopping short of firing the employee or taking any other tangible actions against her in response to her resistance."[133]

This question was carefully examined in the case of *Bundy v. Jackson*.[134] In this case, the D.C. Circuit Court of Appeals considered the claim of a woman who alleged that her rejections of unsolicited and offensive sexual advances from several supervisors in her agency caused those supervisors to unjustifiably delay and block job promotions to which she was entitled.[135] The woman alleged that the "sexually stereotyped insults and demeaning propositions to which she was ... subjected ... caused her anxiety and debilitation."[136] In this case, the employee had complained to her supervisor's supervisor of the harassment, whose response was that "any man in his right mind would want to rape you."[137]

In this case the evidence indicated that the woman's supervisors did "not take the 'game' of sexually propositioning female employees 'seriously,' and the plaintiff's rejection of their advances did *not* evoke in them any motive to take [job related] action against her."[138]

The court then considered what it termed "the novel question" of whether the sort of sexual harassment the woman had suffered here amounted to sex discrimination with respect to the *"terms, conditions, or privileges of employment."*[139] In this case, the court recognized that:

> unless [the current law was extended], an employer could sexually harass a female employee with impunity by carefully stopping short of firing the employee or taking any other tangible actions against her in response to her resistance, thereby creating the impression—the one received by the District Court in this case—that the employer did not take the ritual of harassment and resistance "seriously."[140]

The court then noted that:

> ... so long as women remain inferiors in the employment hierarchy, they may have little recourse against harassment beyond the legal

recourse [the plaintiff] seeks in this case. *The law may allow a woman to prove that her resistance to the harassment cost her her job or some economic benefit, but this will do her no good if the employer never takes such tangible actions against her.*

And this, in turn, means that so long as the sexual situation is constructed with enough coerciveness, subtlety, suddenness, or one-sidedness to negate the effectiveness of the woman's refusal, or so long as her refusals are simply ignored while her job is formally undisturbed, she is not considered to have been sexually harassed.[141]

The court, in recognition of this problem, extended existing law to provide that "sexual harassment, even if it does not result in the loss of tangible job benefits, [may constitute] *illegal sex discrimination.*"[142]

QUESTION: Are sexual flirtations actionable sexual harassment?
ANSWER: As discussed above, the Supreme Court held in *Vinson* that sexual harassment in the workplace must be "sufficiently severe or pervasive 'to alter the conditions of [the victim's] employment and create an abusive working environment.'" Case law, for the most part, has respected this common sense approach of trying to distinguish the legitimate from the claims of the hypersensitive which are often asserted.

In case of *Jones v. Flagship Inc.,*[143] a federal court of appeals considered the claim of a woman attorney who had been hired by a company as a manager of the Equal Employment Opportunity Programs department of that company. She claimed that, among other things, her supervisor, the director of personnel, subjected her to sexual harassment by suggesting to her, one evening on an out-of-town business trip, that she "needed the comfort of a man."[144] She apparently experienced one similar "proposition" on another out-of-town trip. Later, the woman was apparently offended by the presentation of bare-breasted mermaids as table decorations at an office Christmas party.

In rejecting the plaintiff's claim that she had been sexually harassed, the Court observed that the plaintiff had failed to demonstrate that the incidents of which she complained resulted in a tangible job detriment.[145] Accordingly, there was no evidence of quid pro quo harassment.

In rejecting the plaintiff's claim that she had sustained *hostile work environment* harassment, the court offered this explanation:

We conclude ... that while an employee need not prove tangible job detriment to establish a sexual harassment claim, the absence of such detriment requires a commensurately higher showing that the sexually harassing conduct was pervasive and destructive of the working environment. ...

This court [has] held that the state of psychological well-being is a term, condition, or privilege of employment within the meaning of Title VII: "One can readily envision *working environments so heavily polluted with discrimination as to destroy completely the emotional and psychological stability of minority group workers.*" (citation) However, the *"mere utterance of an ethnic or racial epithet which engenders offensive feelings in any employee" does not affect the terms, conditions or privileges of employments to a sufficiently significant degree to violate Title VII.* (citation) "Whether sexual harassment at a workplace is sufficiently severe and persistent to affect seriously the psychological well-being of an employee is a question to be determined with regard to the totality of the circumstances." (citation)[146]

The court found that the evidence supporting plaintiff's charges of sexual harassment was "insufficiently pervasive to constitute a violation of Title VII."[147]

Hostile Environment Sexual Harassment

QUESTION: What type of conduct has been recognized as constituting hostile work environment sexual harassment?

ANSWER: Many different types of conduct have been recognized as constituting hostile environment sexual harassment. The general standard for measuring this type of claim is set forth in *Vinson,* discussed above. The following discussion concerns a case which found this type of harassment to exist.

In *Zabkowicz v. West Bend Co.,*[148] the plaintiff brought a claim under Title VII alleging that she had been harassed by her coworkers. The evidence indicated that one or more of her coworkers had (1) asked if she was wearing a bra; (2) exposed their buttocks to her; (3) addressed her by such terms as "slut," "bitch," and "fucking cunt"; (4) posted numerous pictures of naked women around the warehouse in which she worked which often had the plaintiff's initials inscribed, as well as posting drawings of the plaintiff depicting her engaged in oral sex. In addition, while the plaintiff was pregnant and under a twenty-five-pound lifting restriction, one of her coworkers allegedly "grabbed his crotch and remarked (to the plaintiff), 'I bet you'd have trouble handling this twenty-five-pounder.'"[149]

The evidence indicated that, as a result of such harassment, the plaintiff became anxious, subject to crying spells, and suffered from diarrhea, vomiting, severe nausea and cramping. Her physician diagnosed this illness as "psychophysiological gastrointestinal disease due to harassment at work."[150]

The defendants' contention that the plaintiff was not harassed because of her sex but, rather, because of a "personality clash" was rejected by the court, which explained:

> In my opinion, the defendants' position misinterprets the requirement that a plaintiff show that she was harassed "because of" her sex. There was overwhelming evidence that the plaintiff's colleagues resorted to coarse conduct of a sexual nature in regard to [her]; the sexually offensive conduct and language used would have been almost irrelevant and would have failed entirely in its crude purpose had the plaintiff been a man. I do not hesitate to find that but for her sex, the plaintiff would not have been subjected to the harassment she suffered.[151]

The court next explained that:

> Title VII also requires a showing by the plaintiff that the alleged sexual harassment unreasonably interfered with her work performance or created in intimidating, hostile or offensive working environment. The *requirement that the harassment be unreasonable assures that Title VII does not serve as a vehicle for vindicating the petty slights suffered by the hypersensitive.* The sustained, malicious and brutal harassment meted out to [the plaintiff], however, was more than merely unreasonable; it was malevolent and outrageous. Title VII prohibits precisely such psychologically damaging conditions of employment as were forced upon [the plaintiff].[152]

QUESTION: What are some examples of cases where hostile environment sexual harassment has not been recognized by a court of law?

ANSWER: As with "quid pro quo" cases, many different types of sexually "related" conduct at the workplace will not constitute hostile environment harassment. The following discussion concerns a case which found an employee's charge of hostile environment harassment to be *without* merit.

In *Scott v. Sears Roebuck and Co.,*[153] a woman brought a claim for Title VII violations based on alleged sexual harassment at work. The basis for her claim was that her coworkers supposedly (1) propositioned her (although she admitted that they "never touched her, made a lewd comment to her or explicitly asked her for sex"); (2) "flirted" with her; (3) asked to "take her out" (which *she* interpreted as a request for sex); and (4) when asking for help, would be asked, "What will I get for this?" Although the plaintiff interpreted this last statement as an "obvious request for sex," the evidence indicated that her coworkers never refused to help her for not getting "something in return."[154] The plaintiff alleged that she found the work environment "very uncomfortable."[155]

In finding that the alleged harassment was *not* severe enough to establish a Title VII violation, the court explained:

> Case precedent on establishing a hostile environment can teach that not all sexual harassment is severe or pervasive enough to constitute such a violation. [As one court] stated, the "mere utterance of an ethnic or racial epithet which engenders offensive feelings in an employee" does not affect the terms, conditions, or privileges of employment to a sufficiently significant degree to violate Title VII.
>
> Similarly [another court] emphasized: *Title VII is not a clean language act* and it does not require employers to extirpate all signs of centuries-old prejudices.
>
> Unquestionably the conduct [the plaintiff] complains of falls short of the severity and pervasiveness necessary to constitute an actionable hostile environment. It requires only a reading of [the cases] to see the shocking and pervasive conduct they portray finds no parallel in the climate at [the plaintiff's job]. Apart from an isolated incident with [one] co-worker, [she] was not subjected to vulgarity, demeaning comments, improper inquiries about her private behavior or explicit propositions.[156]

Chapter V

Sexual Orientation Discrimination (Rights of Gay Males and Lesbians)

Employment Discrimination

Introduction

In spite of the increasing acceptance of the lifestyles of gay males and lesbians that seems to be occurring in many quarters of society, it remains all too commonplace for employers to make personnel decisions on the basis of an individual's sexual orientation. This section discusses the scope and extent of the legal protection afforded to gay males and lesbians that may prohibit such discrimination. The complementary rights of employers or prospective employers to use sexual orientation as a basis for making personnel decisions are also discussed. A survey of this area suggests that gays and lesbians are not well protected by the legal system in 1990.

In considering the rights of gay males and lesbians in the workplace, a distinction in law has been made between the rights afforded in public sector employment and the rights afforded in private sector employment. In the public sector, gay males and lesbians may be protected, to a certain extent, by the due process and equal protection clauses of the Constitution. In the private sector, however, such constitutional protection is generally nonexistent and gay males and lesbians must seek other avenues of protection. Fortunately for gays and lesbians, some local governments (and at least one state) have enacted legislation or ordinances prohibiting sexual orientation–based employment discrimination. The gay community and its supporters continue to strive to make such legislation widespread.

Private Sector Employment

QUESTION: What is meant by the "employment-at-will" doctrine?
ANSWER: The employment-at-will doctrine generally gives employers in the private sector the right to fire their employees without cause in the absence of a written employment agreement (which might otherwise limit the circumstances of termination).

QUESTION: Are there any statutory prohibitions that regulate an employer's freedom under the employment-at-will doctrine?
ANSWER: Although there are federal, state, and local statutes that regulate an employer's freedom to use sex as a factor in an employment decision,[1] none of these laws have had, to date, any marked impact on a private employer's ability to discriminate against gay males and lesbians.

Although courts are generally prepared to regulate an employment-at-will relationship by limiting an employer's right to terminate employees when such termination violates "public policy," it does not appear that any court has yet found that an employer's decision to terminate a gay or lesbian employee, because of the employee's sexual orientation, is a violation of such public policy.

QUESTION: If an employer explicitly takes a position condemning sexual orientation discrimination, for instance in an employment handbook, can such statements limit the applicability of the "employment-at-will" doctrine?
ANSWER: It is possible that such statements may have the force of a "written contract"—which could create additional rights for gay males and lesbians and limit an employer's freedom under the otherwise applicable employment-at-will doctrine.

Although no case has been located that has tested the impact of an employer's stated position condemning sexual orientation discrimination, at least one federal court has decided that statements in employee handbooks can be as binding as an express written contract. In the event that such a contract is deemed to exist (i.e., implied by law), that "contract" would control the employment relationship instead of the employment-at-will doctrine. By implication, to the extent an employer makes a statement in an employee handbook condemning discrimination based on sexual orientation, the employer *may* become "bound" by such statement and thereafter precluded from practicing such discrimination — in spite of the employment-at-will doctrine.

In *Joachim v. AT&T Information Systems,*[2] a federal court of appeals considered whether an employer's statements in a company handbook that it would not discriminate on the basis of sexual orientation constituted an explicit contractual agreement, and so modifying an otherwise apparent employee-at-will relationship. In this case, the court found that Texas law, which was applicable in this case, required an "express reciprocal agreement" (i.e., formal contract) in order to modify the employee-at-will doctrine.[3] Accordingly, because the employer's statement was not made in or as part of a contractual agreement, the court found that it could not be bound by its promise not to discriminate against gay males or lesbians on the basis of their sexual orientation.

Significantly, *the same court* that decided *Joachim* found, only one year later (in a different context which did *not* involve statements condemning sexual orientation–based employment discrimination), that statements in employee manuals *may* indeed constitute express written contracts under Texas law.[4] This latter decision suggests that the decision in *Joachim* may now be outdated and that it may already be the law, in some parts of the country, that an employer's statements in an employment manual condemning sexual orientation–based employment discrimination may be binding on that employer and operate to preclude the employer from terminating a gay male or lesbian employee's employment on the basis of that individual's sexual orientation.

> QUESTION: Does Title VII of the 1964 Civil Rights Act prohibit private employers from discriminating on the basis of sexual orientation?
>
> ANSWER: Title VII does not currently afford gays and lesbians protection in the private employment context.

Title VII, which is discussed at some length in Chapter 4, is a federal law which prohibits employment discrimination by both private and public employers on the basis of race, color, religion, sex, and national origin. It does not, however, currently prohibit sexual orientation–based employment discrimination. Although legislation has been introduced in the past to amend Title VII in order to prohibit sexual orientation discrimination, such legislation has never been enacted.[5]

Notwithstanding Title VII's failure to specifically establish gay males and lesbians as "protected classes," a number of lawsuits have been brought which sought to convince courts to "judicially expand" this federal statute to provide such protection. It does not appear that any court has, to date, accepted these invitations to expand Title VII to establish sexual orientation as a forbidden basis for making employment decisions.

For example, in *DeSantis v. Pacific Telephone and Telegraph Co.,*[6] a federal court of appeals considered the claims which several gay males and lesbians had asserted against their respective employers or former employers for discriminating against them because of their sexual orientation. One of the plaintiffs alleged that he was fired as a teacher from a nursery school because he wore a small gold ear loop to school prior to the commencement of the school year. Another individual alleged that he was not hired by another defendant because the employment supervisor concluded that he was gay. Another individual plaintiff alleged that he was continually harassed by his coworkers and had to quit his job to preserve his health because his supervisors did nothing to prevent such harassment. The plaintiffs all alleged that the discrimination which they suffered in their employment violated Title VII, which, they argued, prohibited certain employment discrimination on the basis of sex. The plaintiffs argued that sexual preference is a "sub-category" of "sex" under Title VII and so constituted a protected class of workers, entitled to protection from employment discrimination.[7]

The court of appeals rejected the plaintiff's contention and concluded that "Title VII's prohibition of 'sex discrimination' applies only to discrimination on the basis of gender and should not be judicially extended to include sexual preference such as homosexuality."[8] The court also explained that construing Title VII to prohibit discrimination against homosexuals would "achieve by judicial 'construction' what Congress did not do and has consistently refused to do on many occasions. It would violate the rule that our duty in construing a statute is to 'ascertain ... and give effect to the legislative will.'"[9]

> QUESTION: Are there state or local laws which prohibit sexual orientation–based employment discrimination?
>
> ANSWER: Some states and localities have enacted laws or ordinances prohibiting sexual orientation discrimination in the private employment sector. The interested reader should consult an attorney to determine whether such

state or local laws exist in the area of his or her employment.

At least one state and several local governments have chosen to afford gay males and lesbians greater protection in the private employment sector through the enaction of a statute or ordinance. The state of Wisconsin, for example, has enacted a statute which prohibits sexual orientation–based employment discrimination in the private employment sector.[10] The Wisconsin statute provides, in relevant part, that employment discrimination may be established when "any employer ... refuse[s] to hire, employ, admit or license, or ... bar[s] or terminate[s] from employment ... any individual, or ... discriminate[s] against an individual in promotion, compensation or in terms, conditions or privileges of employment because of the individual's sexual orientation."[11]

In addition, a number of cities and counties across the United States have also enacted ordinances and regulations which prohibit sexual orientation–based employment discrimination. Some of these cities include Tucson, Arizona; Los Angeles, California; Chicago, Illinois; New York City, New York; Seattle, Washington; and the District of Columbia.[12] It remains to be seen how effective these local ordinances and regulations will be in protecting gay males and lesbians in the private employment sector.

QUESTION: Do other state laws, which are *not* specifically designed to prohibit employment discrimination, offer legal protection to gay males and lesbians from sexual orientation–based employment discrimination?

ANSWER: Depending on the circumstances, victims of such discrimination may, among other things, possibly have legal recourse against their employers for (1) the wrongful invasion of their privacy; (2) the wrongful infliction of emotional distress; and (3) their wrongful discharge. Historically, such claims have been difficult to prove. The interested reader should discuss the merits of such claims with their attorney.

Public Sector Employment

Employment in the Military

QUESTION: What is the attitude of the United States military on the employment of gay males and lesbians?

ANSWER: Currently, the Department of Defense guidelines generally require the discharge of individuals who engage or have engaged in homosexual acts.

The Department of Defense's current guidelines require the discharge of individuals who have engaged in homosexual acts, who admit that they are homosexual (or bisexual), or those who seek to marry a member of the same sex.[13]

QUESTION: Do these military regulations include acts that occurred prior to employment by the military?
ANSWER: Yes.

The regulations provide that these proscribed acts are grounds to discharge individuals from the military even though such actions occurred prior to military service.[14]

In this regard, it is noted that the Department of Defense regulations also provide that gay males or lesbians in the service may be discharged for "fraudulent enlistment." Fraudulent enlistment generally refers to an individual's failure to disclose his or her sexual orientation at the time of enlistment.[15]

A recent lawsuit challenged the military's right to discharge a gay service person for fraudulent enlistment. In *Rich v. Secretary of the Army*,[16] a federal court of appeals considered the case of an army medical specialist who challenged his involuntary discharge from the army. The army had honorably discharged the plaintiff for fraudulent enlistment when it learned that, in the enlistment process, he falsely represented that he was not gay.[17] Among other things, the plaintiff claimed that his discharge violated his substantive due process rights, his constitutional right to privacy, his First Amendment rights, and his rights under the equal protection component of the Fifth Amendment of the U.S. Constitution.[18]

In reviewing the record, the court found sufficient evidence to establish that the plaintiff's denials of his homosexuality in the enlistment process were not truthful [i.e., fraudulent].[19] With respect to the plaintiff's claim that his liberty interests in protecting his good name and reputation and his freedom to take advantage of other employment opportunities were infringed,[20] the court noted that "the plaintiff himself [and not the government] publicized his homosexuality and the circumstances of his discharge."[21]

With respect to the plaintiff's claim that his discharge violated his rights to substantive due process because his military record was excellent and there had been no showing of a connection between his homosexuality and his unsuitability for service in the army, the court found that the army's justification for its policy of not permitting gay males or lesbians to enlist was sufficient to defeat this claim. The court explained that

> In the instant case, the Army offered numerous justifications for its policy of not permitting homosexuals to enlist. Among other things, evidence from defense witnesses was offered to show that homosexuals in the service would be detrimental to good order, discipline, morale and military effectiveness because: (1) servicemen must live closely together, and forcing heterosexuals to live and work with homosexuals would produce friction; (2) permitting homosexuals in the military would decrease its prestige and image resulting in an adverse impact on recruiting. In our view, these justifications are sufficient to sustain the Army's policy against a substantive due process attack.[22]

With respect to the plaintiff's claim that his "right to privacy" had been violated by the discharge, the court noted that even assuming that the constitutional right of privacy protects some private consensual homsexual activity, "it does not follow that the army could not exclude homosexuals." The court explained that "the government has a compelling interest in maintaining a strong military force" and "if the army were unable to exclude homosexuals it would 'severely compromise the government's ability to maintain such a force.'"[23]

With respect to the plaintiff's claim that his First Amendment right (to meet with homosexuals and to discuss problems, advocate changes, etc.) had been infringed, the court decided that "plaintiff was not discharged for advocating homosexuality or merely associating with homosexuals. Rather the army discharged him because during enlistment he falsely denied having engaged in homosexual activity."[24] In addition, the court found that "any incidental effect that the army policy of excluding homosexuals has on First Amendment rights is 'justified by the special needs of the military.'"[25] [Other court decisions have indicated that a mere declaration of homosexuality—without proof of homosexual conduct—might prohibit discharge under the First Amendment.][26] The court explained that "[t]o insure that the armed services are always capable of performing their mission, the military must insist upon a respect for duty and a discipline without counterpart in civilian life."[27]

Finally, with respect to the plaintiff's claims that the army's policy of excluding homosexuals violated his equal protection rights under U.S. Constitution's Fifth Amendment, the court, among other reasons, found that the army's sexual orientation based classification is a valid one in light of a compelling governmental interest in maintaining the discipline and morale of the armed forces.[28]

QUESTION: Do service persons discharged on the grounds of homosexuality receive an honorable or dishonorable discharge?

ANSWER: Such individuals generally receive an honorable or general discharge unless the homosexual act(s) occurred under "aggravating circumstances."

The Department of Defense guidelines provide that homosexual acts committed under the following circumstances may be grounds for issuing an "Other than Honorable" discharge:

1. Acts involving the use of force, coercion, or intimidation;
2. Acts with a person under sixteen years of age;
3. Acts with a subordinate in circumstances that violate customary military superior-subordinate relationships;
4. Acts committed openly in public view;
5. Acts committed for compensation;
6. Acts committed aboard a military vessel or aircraft; or
7. Acts committed in another military location subject to military control under aggravating circumstances that have an adverse impact on discipline, order, or morale.[29]

QUESTION: Do the Department of Defense guidelines provide any exceptions to the discharge based on homosexual acts?

ANSWER: The guidelines currently provide the following three exceptions to discharge:

1. If the homosexual act is found to have been uncharacteristic behavior for that individual and the following conditions are met:[30]

   a. Such conduct under all the circumstances is unlikely to recur;
   b. Such conduct was not accomplished by use of force, coercion, or intimidation by the member during a period of military service;
   c. Under the particular circumstances of the

case, the member's continued presence in the
Service is consistent with the interest of the
Service in proper discipline, good order, and
morale; and

d. The member does not desire to engage in or
intend to engage in homosexual acts.

2. When a declaration of homosexual orientation
is false;[31] and

3. When a same-sex marriage (or attempted marriage) is found to be an attempt to avoid or
terminate service in the military.[32]

Public Employment Requiring a Security Clearance

QUESTION: Are gay males and lesbians protected against discrimination in jobs which require security clearances?

ANSWER: It appears that rights of gay males and lesbians are
little different in this area of public employment and
that the FBI and CIA generally deny security clearance
to all persons known to have committed homosexual
acts.[33]

Employment in the Civil Service

QUESTION: Do gay or lesbian employees in the Civil Service sector
have greater protection against discharge based on
sexual orientation than individuals employed in the
military or in positions requiring security clearance?

ANSWER: Some courts have held that before a Civil Service employer may discharge a gay or lesbian individual based
on the individual's sexual orientation, the Service must
establish a rational relationship between that individual's sexual orientation and job efficiency.

One of the leading case precedents in this area of law is *Norton v.
Macey*.[34] In this case, the D.C. Circuit Court of Appeals considered the
claim of a civil service employee at NASA that he should be reinstated
following his discharge for "immoral conduct" involving the making of
an alleged homosexual advance.[35]

In finding that an alleged homosexual advance by a public civil service employee was *not* sufficient to justify dismissal, the court observed:

We are not prepared to say that the Commission could not reasonably
find appellant's homosexual advance to be "immoral," "indecent," or

"notoriously disgraceful" under dominant conventional norms. *But the notion that it could be an appropriate function of the federal bureaucracy to enforce the majority's conventional codes of conduct in the private lives of its employees is at war with elementary concepts of liberty, privacy, and diversity.* And whatever we may think of the Government's qualifications to act *in loco parentis* in this way, the statute precludes from discharging protected employees except for a reason related to the efficiency of the service. Accordingly, a finding that an employee has done something immoral or indecent could support a dismissal without further inquiry only if all immoral or indecent acts of an employee have some ascertainable deleterious effect on the efficiency of the service.[36]

The *Norton* rationale has since been adopted in the *Federal Personnel Manual*. This manual now recognizes that an employee is not automatically disqualified from holding federal employment merely because such individual is gay or lesbian. Some exceptions have, however, been carved out from this general rule. For example, an individual's notoriously disgraceful conduct "can provide a rational relationship between an employee's sexual orientation and his or her job efficiency."[37]

QUESTION: Have constitutional challenges to sexual orientation discrimination based on alleged violations of the Equal Protection Clause of the Constitution met with success?

ANSWER: Generally not.

Courts that have considered whether a public employer's discrimination against an employee based on that employee's sexual orientation have generally found that such discrimination does not violate the Equal Protection Clause of the Constitution.[38]

QUESTION: Does the First Amendment offer protection to gay or lesbian individuals in the public employment sector?

ANSWER: Where individuals allege they have a First Amendment right to declare their homosexual orientation or desire, courts generally seek to balance the government's interest in discharging the individual against the burden on that individual's right to free speech. Some cases have turned on whether the complaining individual has simply indicated their homosexual orientation or, rather, committed homosexual acts.

Criminal Laws Affecting
Gays and Lesbians

Introduction

Many state governments and their citizens believe that same-sex sexual activity is sinful, unnatural, or a crime against nature and society. In an attempt to prohibit such activity, many states have enacted legislation which makes same-sex sexual activity illegal. As a practical matter, these laws may be difficult to enforce. This section addresses the scope and legality of these laws.

Constitutionality of Sodomy Laws

QUESTION: What is meant by the term "sodomy"?
ANSWER: The term "sodomy" generally refers to oral sex (i.e., oral-genital sex) and anal sex (i.e., anal-genital sex).

QUESTION: What is the current status of sodomy in the United States?
ANSWER: Sodomy is currently a crime in a number of states.[39]

QUESTION: Have sodomy statutes withstood federal constitutional challenge?
ANSWER: Yes. The Supreme Court has held that there is no federal constitutional right to engage in private, consensual, same-sex sodomy.

In *Bowers v. Hardwick,*[40] the Supreme Court considered a constitutional challenge to a Georgia sodomy statute that, in relevant part, criminalized consensual same-sex sodomy.[41] The Court first noted that its prior decisions concerning the "right of privacy," which protects, among other things, a woman's right to have an abortion and access to contraceptives, had not construed the Constitution "to confer a right of privacy that extends to homosexual sodomy."[42] The court explained its distinction between other protected privacy interests and same-sex sexual activity by simply noting that there was "no connection between family, marriage or procreation, on the one hand and homosexual activity on the other."[43] The Court then observed that sodomy was a criminal offense in the original thirteen states when the Bill of Rights was ratified, that through 1961, all fifty states had outlawed sodomy, and at the time of the Court's decision in 1986, twenty-four states and the District of Columbia continued to provide criminal penalties for sodomy.[44] Accordingly, the Court rejected the contention that the right to engage in such conduct is "deeply rooted in the Nation's history and tradition."[45] In rejecting the argument that voluntary sexual conduct between consenting adults which occurs in the privacy of a house is protected, the Court explained that illegal conduct is not immunized simply because it occurs in the home.[46]

Finally, in rejecting the assertion that there must be a rational basis for the law and "there is none in this case other than the presumed belief of a majority of the electorate in Georgia that homosexual sodomy is immoral and unacceptable," the Supreme Court simply replied that the law "is constantly based on notions of morality" and such basis is insufficient grounds to invalidate laws under the Due Process Clause of the U.S. Constitution.[47]

QUESTION: Do state sodomy statutes violate the protection afforded by state constitutions?

ANSWER: It is possible that some state constitutions may afford protection and invalidate their state sodomy laws.

The Supreme Court noted in the *Hardwick* decision that its holding (that the U.S. Constitution did not require invalidation of the Georgia sodomy statute) did not limit the protection a state may choose to afford to its citizens by either repealing sodomy laws or invalidating such laws on state constitutional grounds.[48] Some state courts have already accepted the Supreme Court's invitation to strike down a state's sodomy statutes on state constitutional grounds.[49] Whether such challenges will have a widespread impact in the future remains to be seen.

Gay and Lesbian Couples' Right to Marry

Introduction

The institution of marriage throughout the United States has been granted a special legal status by the Supreme Court. For example, in the landmark case of *Loving v. Virginia,*[50] the Supreme Court, striking down a Virginia state law that prohibited marriages between persons of different races, emphasized that marriage is a "'basic civil right of man,' fundamental to our very existence and survival."[51] Although this fundamental right is well-recognized in heterosexual marriages, the same cannot be said about same-sex marriages. This section discusses the current status of laws which purport to regulate the marriage of same-sex couples.

QUESTION: May states make same-sex marriages illegal?
ANSWER: Yes.

QUESTION: What are some of the reasons states use in prohibiting same-sex marriages?
ANSWER: Typical justifications include (1) the impact of same-sex marriages upon procreation and (2) the promotion of traditional societal values (and, impliedly, a refusal to sanction conduct that many find immoral and pernicious).

QUESTION: Have these prohibitions against same-sex marriages been challenged and, if so, on what grounds and with what results?
ANSWER: Challenges have been made on the various grounds including alleged violations of the U.S. Constitution and state equal rights amendments. These challenges have typically proved unsuccessful.

Refusal to Grant Marriage License
Does Not Violate the U.S. Constitution

At least one court has determined that a state's refusal to grant a marriage license to persons of the same sex does not violate the U.S. Constitution. In *Adams v. Howerton*,[52] a federal district court considered a claim brought by a male Australian citizen and male American citizen who went through a purported marriage ceremony in order that the Australian could seek permanent resident status as an immediate relative of an American citizen (a *much* faster process than if such relation is not established). The claim alleged that the Immigration and Naturalization Service had improperly denied the Australian "immediate relative status."[53]

The court summarized the plaintiff's argument as follows:

Plaintiffs argue that some persons are allowed to marry and their union is given full recognition and constitutional protection even though the [purported] justification — procreation — is not possible. They point to marriages being sanctioned between couples who are sterile because of age or physical infirmity, and between couples who make clear that they have chosen not to have children. Plaintiffs go on to claim that sanctioning such unions within the protection of legal marriage, while excluding their union, constitutes an illegal discrimination against them.[54]

The court rejected this argument, and upheld the position taken by the INS. It offered the following explanation:

In my view, if the classification of the group who may validly marry is overinclusive, it does not affect the validity of the classification. In traditional equal protection terminology, it *seems beyond dispute that the state has a compelling interest in encouraging and fostering procreation of the race and providing status and stability to the environment in which children are raised.* This has always been one of society's paramount goals. There is no real alternative to some overbreadth in achieving this goal. The state has chosen to allow legal marriage as between all couples of opposite sex. The alternative would be to inquire of each couple, before issuing a marriage license, as to their plans for children and to give sterility tests to all applicants, refusing licenses to those found sterile or unwilling to raise a family. Such tests and inquiries would themselves raise serious constitutional questions.[55]

Refusal to Grant Marriage License Found Not to Violate State's Equal Rights Amendment

In *Singer v. Hara,*[56] a Washington court considered a claim brought by two male men, who sought to become married but were denied a marriage license, that the Washington law which prohibited same-sex marriages was, among other things, a violation of the state's equal rights amendment which provided, in relevant part, that "Equality of Rights . . . under the law shall not be denied or abridged on account of sex."[57]

In rejecting this claimed violation, the Washington court explained:

The [state] ERA does not create any new rights or responsibilities, such as the conceivable right of persons of the same sex to marry one another; rather, it *merely insures that existing rights and responsibilities, or such rights and responsibilities as may be created in the future, which previously might have been wholly or partially denied to one sex or to the other, will be equally available to members of either sex. . . .*

In the instant case, it is apparent that the state's refusal to grant a license allowing the appellants to marry one another is not based upon appellants' status as males, but rather it is based upon the state's recognition that our society as a whole views marriage as the appropriate and desirable forum for procreation and the rearing of children. This is true even though married couples are not required to become parents and even though some couples are incapable of becoming parents and even though not all couples who produce children are married. These, however, are exceptional situations. The fact remains that marriage exists as a protected legal institution primarily because of societal values associated with the propagation of the human race. Further, it is apparent that no same-sex couple offers the possibility of the birth of children by their union. Thus *the refusal of the state to authorize same-sex marriage results from such impossibility of reproduction rather than from an invidious discrimination "on account of sex."*[58]

Alternative Legal Relationships

QUESTION: Have same-sex couples who have been denied the right to marry sought to establish other legal bases for their relationships?

ANSWER: Yes. Perhaps the most interesting approach is through use of the adoption procedure.

QUESTION: How have courts responded to such adoption petitions?

ANSWER: Some cases have approved the practice, others have not.

In what was perhaps a case of first impression, New York State Family Court considered a twenty-two-year-old male's petition to adopt a twenty-six-year-old male, with whom he was having a homosexual relationship, in order to establish a legally cognizable relationship to facilitate inheritance, the handling of insurance policies, etc. In *Matter of Adoption of Adult Anonymous,*[59] a New York Family Court, finding that consensual homosexuality was no longer a crime in the state and that the parties were willing and informed, approved the adoption petition.

Several years later, however, the New York Court of Appeals (the most authoritative court in that state) took a contrary position in a similar situation. In *In re Adoption of Robert Paul P.,*[60] the court of appeals stated that the adoption proceeding is "not a quasi-matrimonial vehicle to provide nonmarried partners with a legal imprimatur for their sexual relationship."[61]

Sexual Orientation as Grounds for Award of Child Custody

It is well-settled that child custody disputes are generally resolved by courts seeking to protect the subject child's "best interest."[62] In determining how a child's best interest will be enhanced by an award of custody to one parent or another, courts are generally free to consider any factor which they deem relevant. How courts consider one parent's sexual orientation is the subject of this section.

> QUESTION: Have courts considered a parent's sexual orientation as a reason to deny custody of a child to gay and lesbian parents?
> ANSWER: Yes.

In *G.A. v. D.A.,*[63] a Missouri court of appeals considered whether a lower court, in a suit for dissolution of a marriage, had properly awarded custody of the parties' child to the father. The mother was an admitted lesbian.[64] The lower court found that "the best interest of [the child] would be served by giving his custody to [the father]," and indicated that the fact that the mother was a lesbian "tipped the scales in favor of [the father]."[65] The mother then challenged this position on appeal.

The appellate court agreed with the lower court's decision, noting that "a court cannot ignore the effect which the sexual conduct of a parent may have on a child's moral development ... there is far more to the welfare of the child than the physical condition of the house in which [he] lives."[66]

> QUESTION: Do all states presume that a gay or lesbian parent should not be awarded custody?
> ANSWER: No.

A number of state courts have determined that merely because a parent is gay or lesbian is insufficient reason for presuming that such parent is unfit to be awarded custody of his or her child.[67] These courts have held that a parent's sexual orientation will not be reason to justify denial of custody to that parent, absent evidence that such sexual orientation would adversely affect the child.[68]

QUESTION: May a gay or lesbian parent be assured of visitation
with his or her child?

ANSWER: Courts generally presume that the noncustodial parent
should have visitation rights as this is usually considered to be in the child's best interest.

Most states recognize that a child's interest is promoted by a continued bond with the noncustodial parent. Such recognition typically
results in the reward of some type of visitation rights by the noncustodial
gay or lesbian parent. It is theoretically possible, but very unlikely as a
practical matter, for a court to conclude that visitation with a gay or lesbian parent may not be in the child's best interest and, to protect the
child, should be denied.

QUESTION: Assuming visitation is not denied, may it be regulated
in order to ensure that a child will not be exposed to
a "gay or lesbian environment"?

ANSWER: Such regulation of visitation is possible.

Although courts are generally not inclined to deny gay or lesbian
parent visitation rights with their children, courts may be receptive to the
notion of regulating such visitation rights. One common example of
such regulation is to prohibit the parent's same-sex companion from being present during the visitation period.[69]

Another example of judicial regulation of a gay or lesbian parent's
conduct during the course of visitation has been to direct a parent not
to take the child to gay or lesbian social activities during the period of
visitation.[70]

Sexual Orientation as Fault Grounds for Divorce — A Footnote

Whether the sexual orientation of a partner to a marriage may be
grounds for divorce in those states which retain traditional "fault"
grounds[71] is a question that can only be considered by reference to the
matrimonial law in a particular state. It is observed that grounds for
divorce are more likely established by homosexual *conduct* than simply
homosexual sympathies. For example, New York's domestic relations

law provides that adultery is "the commission of an act of sexual or deviate sexual intercourse, voluntarily performed by the defendant, with a person other than the plaintiff after the marriage of plaintiff and defendant."[72] New York courts have recognized that an extramarital homosexual act, not simply homosexual status, may be grounds for divorce.[73]

Chapter VI

Individuals with AIDS

AIDS and the Work Environment

Introduction

Surveys report that the majority of individuals with AIDS are between twenty and fifty years old.[1] Many of these individuals are already in the work force or seek entry therein. The impact of AIDS in the workplace poses many complex and divergent concerns—concerns of the employee with AIDS who seeks dignity and the right to earn income, concerns of coworkers who are often afraid of contracting AIDS, and concerns of employers who must consider not only their employees' rights and concerns, but their customers' concerns as well. This section addresses some of the critical issues resulting from the presence of AIDS in the workplace.

Rights of AIDS Infected Employees

Protection from Employment Discrimination

Federal Protection Against AIDS Discrimination

QUESTION: Does federal law prohibit employment discrimination against individuals with AIDS?

ANSWER: Early decisions in this rapidly developing area of law have held that the Federal Rehabilitation Act of 1973[2] prohibits discrimination by certain designated employers (such as recipients of federal funds or federal contractors) against AIDS infected individuals in the workplace.

It is possible that the U.S. Constitution's protection

134

of certain "privacy rights," due process and equal protection may offer some additional protection to covered employees.

The Federal Rehabilitation Act

Title V of the Federal Rehabilitation Act prohibits certain designated categories of employers (such as federal contractors and federal employers) from discriminating against qualified handicapped persons. Protection under the act is generally afforded to individuals who can establish that they are (1) handicapped as defined by the act; (2) otherwise qualified for the position sought; (3) discriminated against in a program or activity which receives federal financial assistance; and (4) discriminated against solely by reason of their handicap.[3]

Section 706(8)(b) of the Federal Rehabilitation Act defines an individual with a handicap to include any "physical or mental impairment which substantially limits one or more of [a] person's major life activities."

The Supreme Court considered the scope of the term "handicapped person" in a case captioned *School Board of Nassau County, Florida v. Arline.*[4] In *Arline,* the Supreme Court was asked to consider whether a school teacher, discharged after suffering a third relapse of tuberculosis within a two-year period, was a handicapped person within the meaning of the Federal Rehabilitation Act. In holding that persons suffering from a contagious disease are handicapped under the Rehabilitation Act, the Supreme Court stated:

> We do not agree with the [School Board] that, in defining a handicapped individual under Section [794] the contagious effects of a disease can be meaningfully distinguished from the diseases' physical effects on a claimant in a case such as this.... It would be unfair to allow an employer to seize upon the distinction between the effects of a disease on others and the effects of a disease on a patient and use that distinction to justify discriminatory treatment.[5]

The Court found that once an individual is determined to be handicapped by a contagious disease, an individualized inquiry must be made to determine whether that person is "otherwise qualified to perform his or her job."[6] Some of the factors which the Supreme Court instructed trial courts to consider in this regard in deciding cases brought under the Federal Rehabilitation Act are (a) the nature of the risk (how the disease is transmitted); (b) the duration of the risk (how long is the carrier infectious); (c) the severity of the risk (what is the potential harm to third parties); and (d) the probabilities the disease will be transmitted and will cause varying degrees of harm.[7]

The Supreme Court's *Arline* decision did not specifically answer the question of whether AIDS constituted a "contagious disease" within the meaning of the Rehabilitation Act. The Court merely observed, in a footnote, that "this case does not present, and we therefore do not reach, the questions whether a carrier of a contagious disease such as AIDS could be considered to have a physical impairment, or whether such a person could be considered, solely on the basis of contagiousness, a handicapped person as defined by the Act."[8]

Only a few lower court decisions have since addressed the question of whether AIDS is a protected handicap under the Federal Rehabilitation Act. The most significant case in this area is probably *Chalk v. United States District Court*,[9] in which the Ninth Circuit Court of Appeals held that a schoolteacher afflicted with AIDS was entitled to a preliminary injunction ordering his reinstatement. The teacher had been reassigned to an administrative position, and barred from teaching in the classroom, upon having been diagnosed as having AIDS. In finding that AIDS is a handicap within the meaning of the Federal Rehabilitation Act, after considering the factors set forth in *Arline,* the Court emphasized that

> There is no known risk of non-sexual infection in most of the situations we encounter in our daily lives. We know that family members living with individuals who have the AIDS virus do not become infected except through sexual contact. There is no evidence of transmission (spread) of AIDS virus by everyday contact even though these family members shared foods, towels, cups, razors, even toothbrushes, and kissed each other.[10]

Rejecting the lower court's position that enough is not known about AIDS to be *completely certain* that it poses no risks to the teacher's students, the appellate court said that such a position "improperly placed an impossible burden of proof on the [teacher]."[11] The court explained that "[l]ittle in science can be proved with complete certainty, and Section 504 does not require such a test." As authoritatively construed by the Supreme Court, Section 504 allows the exclusion of an employee only if there is "a significant risk of communicating an infectious disease to another."[12] The court then ordered his immediate reappointment to his teaching duties. Finally, it is interesting to note the support given to the teacher by his students and their parents — some of whom submitted legal briefs in support of his claims for reinstatement and some of whom greeted him with hugs and gifts upon his return to work.[13]

State Law Protection against AIDS Discrimination

QUESTION: Do state laws prohibit employment discrimination against individuals with AIDS?
ANSWER: Some states prohibit such discrimination.

In addition to the protection which may be afforded to certain employees by the Federal Rehabilitation Act, many states have enacted their own legislation which also prohibits discrimination against the handicapped. Such state laws may provide additional protection against AIDS-based employment discrimination.

The National Gay Rights Advocates conducted a survey on the status of state handicap discrimination laws in 1986.[14] This survey found that the following states (and the District of Columbia) had formally *recommended* the prohibition of AIDS-based discrimination:

> California, Colorado, Connecticut, the District of Columbia, Florida, Illinois, Maine, Massachusetts, Michigan, Minnesota, Missouri, New Jersey, New Mexico, New York, Oregon, Pennsylvania, Rhode Island, Texas, Washington, West Virginia, and Wisconsin.

The following states declared that AIDS-based discrimination is *prohibited:*

> Georgia, Louisiana, Montana, New Hampshire and North Carolina.

The following states stated that they would accept and *investigate* AIDS discrimination complaints:

> Alaska, Delaware, Kansas, Nebraska, Ohio, Tennessee,[15] Vermont, and Wyoming.

The following states have not yet made a determination as to how to treat this subject:

Alabama, Arizona, Arkansas, Hawaii, Idaho, Indiana, Iowa, Maryland, Mississippi, North Dakota, Oklahoma, South Carolina, South Dakota, and Virginia.

In responses to the survey, Kentucky indicated that its handicap statute excluded persons with communicable disease, such as AIDS, from coverage. Utah indicated that it might consider AIDS to be a handicap under certain factual situations, but the mere diagnosis of AIDS would not necessarily trigger protection under Utah law. Nevada did not respond to the survey.

The interested reader is urged to determine the possible existence and applicability of current state or local laws which may prohibit employment discrimination based on AIDS.

> QUESTION: Have any of these state handicap antidiscrimination statutes been tested in a court of law?
> ANSWER: Yes.

The significance of possible state law protection against AIDS-based employment discrimination is demonstrated in a leading decision rendered by the Florida Commission on Human Relations. In the case of *Shuttleworth v. Broward County Office of Budget and Management Policy,*[16] the Florida Commission on Human Relations held that the Florida Human Rights Act, which prohibited discrimination on the basis, among other things, of handicaps,[17] protects an AIDS-inflicted employee from employment discrimination on the basis of that "handicap." This case considered the claim of a budget analyst in the Broward County's Office of Budget and Management Policy who was fired after being diagnosed as having AIDS. In considering the employee's challenge to the dismissal, the Florida Commission reasoned that "based upon the plain meaning of the term 'handicap' and the medical evidence presented, an individual with Acquired Immune Deficiency Syndrome is within the coverage of the Human Rights Act."[18] The Florida Commission held that the employer "failed to show that there was substantial risk of future injury or reasonable basis for its assessment of risk of injury to [the inflicted employee], other employees or the public by retaining [the afflicted employee] in its employ."

This matter was subsequently settled and Shuttleworth was offered reinstatement in his previous job, a continuation of health and life insurance, $196,000 in back pay, as well as reimbursements for medical bills and attorneys' fees. The county also agreed to treat other employees with AIDS as handicapped under federal law.[19]

In *Raytheon Co. v. Fair Employment & Hous. Comm'n.,*[20] an employee diagnosed with AIDS was placed on indefinite medical leave and was refused permission to return to work although he was physically capable of returning to work and wished to do so. The California Fair Employment and Housing Commission found that casual workplace contact with infected employees would not have placed coworkers at the risk of contracting AIDS. The Commission further determined that AIDS is a "physical handicap" because it (eventually) disables its victims. Accordingly, the Commission found the defendant company chargeable with unlawful discrimination of the handicapped for its refusal to permit the AIDS-infected employee to return to work.

In *Isabell v. Sebastian's Restaurant,*[21] a West Virginia Human Rights Commission awarded $50,700 to a waiter who claimed he had been fired because of rumors that he had AIDS. The award was entered to compensate the plaintiff for lost wages, humiliation, emotional and mental stress, and attorneys' fees. In addition, the West Virginia Commission ordered the defendant to rehire the plaintiff.

Miscellaneous State Law Claims
for AIDS-based Employment Discrimination

In addition to the protection which may be offered to AIDS-infected employees under various federal, state and local statutes or ordinances, employees discriminated against because of AIDS may also have certain claims arising out of state tort and contract law. Such claims may, depending on the circumstances, include actions for (1) wrongful discharge; (2) the intentional infliction of emotional distress; (3) defamation; and (4) invasion of privacy. The viability of these claims in legal proceedings generally remains to be determined. The interested reader should discuss the possible application of these claims to his or her situation with their attorney.

Rights of Coworkers

In light of the widely shared, yet incorrect, assumption that AIDS is easily transmitted to others by mere association, it is not uncommon for coworkers of an AIDS victim to be concerned about the possibility of their contracting AIDS through casual contact in the workplace. Some recent surveys suggest that one in four employees claim they would refuse to work with an individual with AIDS.[22] This section considers what rights, if any, such coworkers actually have to bar employees with AIDS from working at their side.

> QUESTION: Can coworkers bar an individual with AIDS from continuing employment?
>
> ANSWER: The few cases which have considered this question have generally indicated that there are less drastic alternatives available to protect coworkers. Courts generally consider both the likelihood of injury to coworkers and the seriousness of possible injury in resolving whether an employer is justified in terminating a handicapped employee's employment. Because it is widely accepted that AIDS is not transmitted by casual contact, coworkers are generally not believed to be at risk of AIDS exposure.

In *Shuttleworth v. Broward County Office of Budget and Management Policy,*[23] the Florida Commission on Human Relations found that Shuttleworth did not have an easily transmittable infection at the time of his termination, that he did not come into contact with a large number of coworkers because he worked in a private office, and that there was no evidence that AIDS could be transmitted to coworkers by casual contact.[24] Accordingly, the Florida Commission on Human Rights determined that the defendant-employer had not established that Shuttleworth posed substantial risk of future injury to his coworkers or to the public.[25]

In *Chalk v. United States District Court,*[26] discussed on p. 136, the Ninth Circuit Court of Appeals noted that courts may establish reasonable procedures, including periodic reports from physicians, to insure that no significant harm will arise to coworkers from employing an AIDS victim.

It is noted that courts which have considered the fears of coworkers arising from other handicaps have often used similar logic (i.e., addressing the likelihood of transmission of a disease to coworkers) in reaching decisions. For example, in *Bev v. Bolger,*[27] a federal district court found that the risk of stroke from an employee's uncontrolled hypertension justified the employer's decision to deny employment to the plaintiff who could not perform essential job functions without endangering the health or safety of others.

In *E.E. Black, Ltd. v. Marshall,*[28] a federal district court held that a federal contractor could not refuse to hire a handicapped worker because of fear of injury to the worker unless the contractor could establish that its decision was necessary to ensure the safe performance of the job.

Because it is now generally accepted that the risk of AIDS transmission in the workplace is not likely to occur by mere association or casual contact, employers may expect to face a heavy burden in justifying their decision to terminate an AIDS-infected employee based on their own fears or on the fears of coworkers.

Employer Defenses

Customer Preference

QUESTION: May employers refuse to hire job applicants with AIDS, or fire employees with AIDS, because they are concerned about public or customer contact?
ANSWER: Probably not.

It remains to be generally determined whether an employer may properly terminate an AIDS-infected employee on the grounds that the employer's customers are concerned about their safety. As noted in Chapter 4, employers are generally unable to defend a sexual discrimination case because of their customers' perceived preference of dealing with members of one sex over another. In light of the evidence that AIDS is not transmissible through casual contact, it would be surprising for courts to uphold an employment decision to terminate an AIDS-infected employee because of customer preference. How courts treat this concern in practice remains to be seen.

Increased Health Care Costs and Absenteeism

QUESTION: May employers refuse to hire job applicants with AIDS, or fire employees with AIDS, because of the potential for high health care costs.
ANSWER: Probably not.

Although it generally remains to be determined whether employers may terminate AIDS-infected employees because of the employers' expectation that such employees will incur significant health care costs, it is anticipated that such justification will be found unacceptable by the courts. The Employee Retirement Income Security Act of 1974 (ERISA) provides that it is unlawful for an employer to discharge or discriminate against a participant or beneficiary of an employee benefit plan "for the purpose of interfering with the attainment of any right to which such participant may become entitled under the plan."[29] The provision, as interpreted, means that the potential cost of an employee's health care plan cannot be the basis for an employment decision affecting that employee. The provision has already been considered in the context of an employee who was discharged upon his employer's learning that he had multiple sclerosis. The employer believed that this disease would significantly add to the cost of the company's health and welfare plan. Rejecting the employer's defense, a federal district court awarded the discharged employee $475,000.[30] Accordingly, precedent exists which suggests that an employer will not be permitted to discriminate against an AIDS-infected employee on the grounds that that employee may become an economic burden to the employer.

Employment Related AIDS Testing

QUESTION: Do tests exist which can detect the HIV virus?
ANSWER: There are some tests. The most popular AIDS test is known as ELISA—the enzyme link immuno sorbent assay test. Typically, if an individual tests positive under this test, a second test, known as the Western Blot test, is performed, as confirmation. These tests may detect the HIV virus but will not necessarily confirm whether the individual with such virus will ever suffer from AIDS. The reliability of such tests is subject to challenge.

QUESTION: Do employers utilize such testing in screening job applicants?
ANSWER: Other than the military, it does not appear that AIDS testing is generally used by prospective employers screening job applicants.

QUESTION: Have any states passed laws regulating the use of AIDS testing as a condition of employment?
ANSWER: Currently, such states as California,[31] Florida,[32] Massachusetts,[33] and Wisconsin[34] prohibit AIDS testing as the basis for forming an employment decision about an individual. In addition, a number of cities have passed

local ordinances which also prohibit such employment related AIDS testing. These cities include San Francisco, Los Angeles and Denver, Colorado.

QUESTION: Are government employment decisions further restricted by federal constitutional protection?

ANSWER: It is possible that the Fourth Amendment protection against unreasonable searches or seizures may preclude AIDS testing. To date, conflicting decisions have been rendered on the subject.[35]

QUESTION: Does an employee have a right to keep the results of his AIDS test private?

ANSWER: It is possible that an employee's privacy is protected by either a state statute[36] or case precedent. The interested reader should investigate this matter further.

QUESTION: Is there a federal constitutional right to privacy associated with AIDS testing?

ANSWER: A threshold requirement for federal constitutional protection is the presence of federal, state, or local government action. [Private employers are generally not bound unless their conduct is related to "government action."] Where applicable, the federal constitution may offer some protection against AIDS testing.[37]

QUESTION: If an employment test determines that an individual has AIDS, does the employer have a responsibility to warn individuals which may be at risk of exposure?

ANSWER: As this area of law continues to develop, the answer to this question should become clearer. On the one hand, with respect to coworkers and others who are not at risk of exposure from casual contact only, an employer risks a lawsuit by the employee for invasion of privacy and defamation upon such disclosure. On the other hand, a failure to disclose might expose the employer to liability for the third party who is at risk. The interested reader is advised to seek professional advice if posed with such a dilemma.

AIDS in the Classroom

Introduction

In February 1986, the nation learned of Ryan White's sad story. Ryan, then a fourteen-year-old boy living in Kokomo, Indiana, was excluded from school because he was found to have AIDS.[38] Although Ryan was readmitted to school after the parents of other children dropped their legal opposition to his attendance (apparently due to high legal fees), his case (and others like his) sparked wide public debate about the rights of innocent children with AIDS to receive an education on the one hand or, on the other hand, the right of innocent classmates to be "protected." This is a developing area of law which squarely places a critical element of a child's development at risk. Courts have long realized that "it is doubtful that any child may reasonably be expected to succeed in life if he is denied the opportunity for an education."[39] How courts address the rights of children with AIDS will surely affect all of us. This section briefly reviews some of the judicial reactions to this question.

QUESTION: Is there a majority position on the question of whether a student with AIDS has a right to attend school or to be excluded from attendance?

ANSWER: Most of the cases which have gone to court appear to recognize a child's right to remain in the classroom unless the student's health does not permit classroom attendance. Only a few reported judicial decisions have been located which, upholding school policies, allow the automatic exclusion of students with AIDS regardless of the risk posed to classmates.[40]

QUESTION: What rationale had been adopted in those decisions permitting students to remain in the classroom?

ANSWER: These decisions are generally based on the evidence that it is virtually impossible to transmit the AIDS virus in the classroom.

A New York State Supreme Court recently had an opportunity to consider the New York City Board of Education Policy concerning children with AIDS. In *District 27 Community School Board v. Board of Education*,[41] the court held that the automatic exclusion from school of all children with AIDS would violate their rights under the Federal Rehabilitation Act and equal protection of the laws.

References

Chapter II

1. 410 U.S. 113 (1973).
2. 102 S. Ct. 3040 (1989).
3. See *N.Y. Times,* July 4, 1989, A11, Col. 1.
4. 410 U.S. 113 (1973).
5. *Id.* at 117. The Court noted that similar statutes were then in existence in a majority of the states. *Id.*
6. *Id.* at 154.
7. *Id.* at 153.
8. *Id.* at 162.
9. *Id.* at 163.
10. *Id.* at 164–64 (emphasis supplied).
11. 448 U.S. 297 (1980).
12. The version of the Hyde Amendment that was challenged in *McRae* is found at Act of Nov. 20, 1979, Pub.L.No. 96-123, Section 109, 93 Stat. 923, 926 (1981).
13. 448 U.S. at 302 (Citing Pub.L. 96-123 Section 109, 93 Stat. 926).
14. *Id.* at 321–25.
15. *Id.* at 316 (emphasis supplied).
16. See, e.g., *Wall St. Journal,* Oct. 13, 1989, A16, Col. 2.
17. 448 U.S. 358 (1980).
18. *Id.* at 368–69.
19. See Relkin and Solomon, *Using State Constitutions to Expand Public Funding for Abortions: Throwing Away the Carrot with the Stick,* 9 Women's Rights Law Reporter, No. 1, 27, 32 N.11 (1986) (citations omitted).
20. *Id.*
21. *Id.*
22. *Id.*
23. *Id.*
24. 432 U.S. 519 (1977).
25. *Id.* at 519.
26. *Id.* at 521.
27. *Id.*
28. 109 S. Ct. 3040 (1989).
29. *Id.* at 3040, citing Mo. Rev. Stat. Section 188.210 and 188.215.

30. *Id.* at 3043.

31. 109 S. Ct. 3040 (1989).

32. *Id.* at 3041–42, citing Mo. Rev. Stat. Section 188.029.

33. *Id.* at 3044, 3054.

34. *Id.*

35. *Id.* at 3058.

36. *Id.*

37. 428 U.S. 52 (1976).

38. *Id.* at 58.

39. *Id.* at 68.

40. *Id.*

41. *Id.* at 68–69.

42. *Id.* at 69.

43. *Id.*

44. 140 Misc.2d 397, 531 N.Y.S.2d 78 (1988).

45. 531 N.Y.S.2d at 79.

46. B. Ryan and E. Plutzer, *When Married Women Have Abortions: Spousal Notification and Marital Interaction,* 51 J. of Marriage & the Family 41, 41–42 n.2 (1989) (reporting that Florida, Illinois, Kentucky, Montana, Nevada, Rhode Island, and Utah currently have "spousal notification" laws).

47. 659 F.2d 476 (S&L Cir. 1981).

48. *Id.* at 479.

49. *Id.* at 483.

50. *Id.* at 486–87.

51. 443 U.S. 622 (1979).

52. *Id.* at 633.

53. *Id.* at 634.

54. *Id.* at 638–39, 642.

55. *Id.* at 642.

56. *Id.* at 643, citing *Planned Parenthood of Central Missouri v. Danforth,* 428 U.S. at 74 (emphasis supplied).

57. *Id.*

58. *Id.* at 643–44.

59. 450 U.S. 398 (1981).

60. *Id.* at 411–12.

61. *Id.* at 413.

62. *Hodgson v. Minnesota,* 58 U.S.L.W. 4957 (1990) and *Ohio v. Akron Center for Reproductive Health,* 58 U.S.L.W. 4979 (1990).

63. See *The Battles in the States Get Fiercer,* The National Law Journal, Dec. 4, 1989, p. 39 (citing survey of American Civil Liberties Union).

64. 111 Misc.2d 532, 444 N.Y.S.2d 545 (1981).

65. 444 N.Y.S.2d at 546.

66. *Id.*

67. *Id.* at 547 (citation omitted).

68. 476 U.S. 747 (1986).

69. *Id.* at 760–61.

70. *Id.* at 761.

71. *Id.* at 762.

72. *Id.* at 763.

73. *Id.*
74. *Id.* at 764.
75. *Id.*
76. *Id.*
77. 462 U.S. 416 (1983).
78. 113 Misc.2d 940, 450 N.Y.S.2d 350 (1982).
79. 450 N.Y.S.2d at 355.
80. *Id.* at 356.
81. *Id.*
82. 109 N.J. 396, 537 A.2d 1227 (N.J. 1988).
83. 537 A.2d at 1235.
84. *Id.*
85. *Id.*
86. *Id.*
87. *Id.* at 1236.
88. *Id.* at 1240, citing N.J.S.A. 9:3–54a.
89. *Id.* at 1241.
90. *Id.* at 1241–42.
91. *Id.* at 1250.
92. *Id.* at 1255 et seq.
93. *Id.* at 1258.
94. 704 S.W.2d 209 (Ky. 1986).
95. *Id.* at 211.
96. Kentucky Revised Statute 199.590(2).
97. 704 S.W.2d at 211.
98. *Id.* at 211–12.
99. *Id.* at 212–13.
100. 132 Misc.2d 972, 505 N.Y.S.2d 813, 818 (Sup. Ct. Nassau Co. 1986).
101. *See, e.g.,* N.Y. Soc. Serv. Law Section 374(6) (McKinney 1977) (permitting only the payment of natural mother's medical expenses). *See also* Pa. Stat. Ann. tit. 18, Section 4305 (Pennsylvania law making it a misdemeanor to "deal in humanity" by trading, bartering, buying, selling, or dealing in infant children).
102. See Ark. Stat. Ann. Title 9, Section 9-10-201 (Supp. 1989). This statute provides:

> (a) Any child born to a married woman by means of artificial insemination shall be deemed the legitimate natural child of the woman and the woman's husband if the husband consents in writing to the artificial insemination.
>
> (b) A child born by means of artificial insemination to a woman who is married at the time of the birth of the child shall be presumed to be the child of the woman giving birth and the woman's husband, *except in the case of a surrogate mother, in which event the child shall be that of:* (1) the biological father and the woman intended to be the mother if the biological father is married; or (2) the biological father only if unmarried; or (3) the woman intended to be the mother in cases of a surrogate mother when an anonymous donor's sperm was utilized for artificial insemination.

(c)(1) A child born by means of artificial insemination to a woman who is unmarried at the time of birth of the child shall be, for all legal purposes, the child of the woman giving birth, *except in the case of a surrogate mother, in which event the child shall be that of:* (1) the biological father and the woman intended to be the mother if the biological father is married; or (2) the biological father only if unmarried; or (3) the woman intended to be the mother in cases of a surrogate mother when an anonymous donor's sperm was utilized for artificial insemination.

(2) *For birth registration purposes, in cases of surrogate mothers,* the woman giving birth shall be presumed to be the natural mother and shall be listed as such on the certificate of birth, but a substituted certificate of birth may be issued upon orders of a court of competent jurisdiction (emphasis supplied).

103. Congressman Luken's proposed bill (HR 2243) is reported at *Surrogate Parenthood: A Legislative Update,* 13 Fam. L. Rep. 1442 (BNA 1987).

104. See S. Liebhaber, *In Re Baby M.,* The Women's Advocate (Vol. IX, No. 2) 1, 6 (April 1988).

105. See e.g., *Mississippi* [Miss. Code Ann. Section 93-9-9 (Supp. 1985)]; and *Nebraska* [Neb. Rev. Stat. Section 43-1411 (1984)].

106. A married surrogate mother may have to overcome a presumption that the child she seeks support for is not her husband's.

107. *Dorland's Illustrated Medical Dictionary* 669 (26th ed. 1981).

108. See, Note, *Artificial Insemination: Donor Rights in Situations Involving Unmarried Recipients,* 26 J. of Fam. L. 793, 794, N.6 (1987–88) (hereinafter "Note — Artificial Insemination").

109. *Id.* at 794.

110. 23 U.S.L.W. 2308 (Ill. Super. Ct. 1954), *app. dis. on procedural grounds,* 12 Ill. App.2d 473, 139 N.E.2d 844 (1956).

111. Ala. Code Section 27-17-12 (1985); Wyo. Stat. Section 14-2-103 (1978).

112. See *Note — Artificial Insemination,* supra, Note 108 at 795–96.

113. See *Sexual Orientation and the Law* (R. Achtenberg, ed.) 1.04 [1] [C] (1989).

114. See Ga. Code Ann. Section 74-101.1(b) (1981); Okla. Stat. Ann. tit. 10, Section 553 (West 1982); Oregon Rev. Stat. Section 667.360 (1979); New York City Health Code, art. 21, Section 21.01.

115. 152 N.J. Super. 160, 377 A.2d 821 (1971).

116. 152 N.J. Super. at 167.

117. 179 Cal. App. 3d 386, 224 Cal. Rptr. 530 (1986).

118. 179 Cal. App. 3d at 389.

119. *Id.*

120. *Id.* at 389–90.

121. *Id.*

122. Cal. Civ. Code Section 7005(B).

123. *Id.* at 394.

124. See *Note — Artificial Insemination,* supra, Note 108 at 805–806.

125. See Curie-Cohen, Luttrell & Shapiro, *Current Practice of Artificial Insemination by Donor in the United States,* 300 New Eng. J. Med. 585, 1301–1303 (1979).

126. I. Sloan, *The Law Governing Abortion, Contraception & Steriliza-tion,* p. 27 (Oceana Publications, Inc. 1988) (hereinafter *Sloan*).

127. Discussed in *Sloan,* Note 126, at pp. 27–28.

128. *Id.*

129. 381 U.S. 479 (1965).

130. *Id.* at 485–86 (emphasis supplied).

131. 405 U.S. 438 (1972).

132. *Id.* at 440–41.

133. *Id.* at 442.

134. *Id.*

135. *Id.* at 453.

136. *Id.* at 453–54 (citations omitted).

137. 431 U.S. 678 (1977).

138. *Id.* at 685, citing *Eisenstadt v. Baird* (discussed above).

139. *Id.* at 686.

140. *Id.* at 687–88.

141. *Id.* at 692.

142. *Id.* at 694.

143. *Sloan,* supra Note 126, at pp. 53–54. See also Kellog, *Legal Aspects of Sex Education,* 26 Am. J. Com. L. 573 (1978).

144. 615 F.2d 1162 (6th Cir. 1980).

145. *Id.* at 1169.

146. *Id.*

147. 51 Cal. App.3d 1, 124 Cal. Rptr. 68 (1975).

148. 51 Cal. App.3d at 18 (citation omitted).

149. Van Dyke, *The Dalkon Shield: A "Primer" in IUD Liability,* 6 W. St. U.L. Rev. 1, 2 n.2 (1978).

150. *In re Northern District of California "Dalkon Shield" IUD Prods. Liab. Ltg.,* 526 F. Supp. 887, 893 (N.D. Cal. 1981), vacated 693 F.2d 897 (9th Cir. 1982), cert. den., 459 U.S. 1171 (1983).

151. *Palmer v. A.H. Robins Co.,* 684 P.2d 187, 187, 210–21. (Colo. 1984)

152. 483 F.2d 237 (10th Cir. 1973).

153. *Id.* at 238–39.

154. *Id.* at 240.

155. 145 Cal. App.3d. 369, 193 Cal. Rptr. 422 (1983).

156. 145 Cal. App.3d at 374.

157. *Id.* at 381 et seq.

158. 443 N.Y.S.2d 343, *aff'd* 451 N.Y.S.2d 766, *aff'd* 462 N.Y.S.2d 819 (1983).

159. 443 N.Y.S.2d at 344.

160. *Id.* at 347–48.

161. 137 Mich. App. 202, 357 N.W.2d 860 (1984).

162. 357 N.W.2d at 861.

163. Sloan, supra, Note 126, at p. 37.

164. A vasectomy is performed by anesthetizing the patient's scrotum, cutting the scrotum to reach the sperm ducts, which are then cut and closed off. The incisions are then stitched and the scars are practically invisible after a couple of weeks. The entire procedure typically takes about 15–20 minutes. See Public Health Service Regulations, 42 C.F.R. 50.210 (1988).

165. A tubal ligation refers to the blocking of a woman's fallopian tubes so that her eggs cannot travel from her ovaries to her uterus. This blocking makes pregnancy impossible. See 42 C.F.R. 50.210 (1988).

166. *Sloan,* supra, Note 126, at p. 38.

167. 42 C.F.R. 50.210 et. seq. (1988).

168. 42 C.F.R. 50.203.

169. Okla. Stat. Ann. Section 200.1

170. See, e.g., Official Code of Ga. 31-20-2.

171. But see *Ponter v. Ponter,* 342 A. 2d 574 (1975) (Married women in N.J. may be sterilized without husband's consent.)

172. *Id.* at 41.

173. Eugenic has been defined as "relating to or fitted for the production of good offspring: relating to or aiming at the improvement of the race or breed." *Webster's Third New International Dictionary.*

174. 274 U.S. 200 (1927).

175. *Id.* at 207.

176. *Id.*

177. Reported at *Wash. Post,* Feb. 23, 1980 at Al, Col. 1.

178. See O'Hara and Sanks *Eugenic Sterilization,* 45 Geo. L.J. 20, 31 (1956).

179. 316 U.S. 535 (1942).

180. *Id.* at 541.

181. H. Clark, *The Law of Domestic Relations in the U.S.* 16, (1968).

182. *Id.*

183. See *DNA — The New Fingerprints,* A.B.A.J. (May 1, 1988) p. 66.

184. *Id.*

185. *Id.*

186. *Id.* at 70.

187. See Note, *The Burden of Proof in a Paternity Action,* 25 J. of Fam. L. 357, 360 (1986–87).

188. 506 A.2d 879 (1986).

189. *Id.* at 882.

190. *Id.* at 882–83.

191. See, e.g. *Angela B. v. Glenn D.,* 126 Misc.2d 646, 482 N.Y.S.2d 971, 978 (Fam. Ct. 1984).

192. 292 S.E.2d 654 (W.Va. 1982).

193. *Id.* at 656 n.3, citing W.Va. Code 48-7-1 et seq.

194. *Id.* at 656.

195. 109 S. Ct. 2333 (1989).

196. No. E-14496 (Circuit Court for Blount County, Tennessee) reported at 1989 Tenn. App. Lexis 641.

197. *Id.*

198. *Id.*

199. *Id.*

200. *Id.*

201. LSA-R.S. 9:121 et seq.

202. Nieburg, Marks, McLaren & Remington, *The Fetal Tobacco Syndrome,* 253 J.A.M.A. 2998 (1985).

203. Reported in the *Wall Street Journal,* July 17, 1989, B8 clm. 6.

204. *Id.*

205. Reported in *The National Law Journal,* May 22, 1989.

206. *Id.*

207. *Id.*

208. Unpublished 1982 case discussed in Parness, *Protection of Potential Human Life in Illinois: Policy & Law at Odds,* 5 N. Ill. U.L. Rev. 1, 20–21 (1984).

209. Discussed in Shaw, *Conditional Prospective Rights of the Fetus,* 5 J. Legal Med. 63, 104–5 (1984). Evidence revealed the mother used large amounts of Quaaludes, Valiums, Morphine and Cocaine. See generally, *Legal Rights and Issues Surrounding Conception, Pregnancy and Birth,* 39 Vand. L. Rev. 597, note 1480 (1986) (hereinafter *Note — Legal Rights*).

210. Discussed in *The National Law Journal,* May 8, 1989, p. 14.

211. *Id.*

212. *Id.*

213. *Id.*

214. Reported in the *Wall Street Journal,* Sept. 18, 1989, p. B6, Col. 4.

215. *State v. Piner,* 10 Fam. L. Rep. (BNA) 1270 (Cal. App. Feb. 17, 1984).

216. *Id.*

217. This case is reported in Bowes & Selgestad, *Fetal v. Maternal Rights: Medical and Legal Perspectives,* 58 Am. J. Obstet. & Gynec. 209, 209–11 (1981).

218. *Id.* at 211.

219. Col. Rev. Stat. Section 19-1-104(3) (1973 & Supp. 1985).

220. *Bowes & Selgestad,* supra Note 217, at 212.

221. See Note — Legal Rights, supra, Note 209, at 834.

222. Discussed in Flanigan, "Fleeing the Law: A Matter of Faith," *Det. Free Press,* June 29, 1982, at 3A [hereinafter *Fleeing the Law*]; Flanigan, "Mom Follows Belief, Gives Birth in Hiding," *Det. Free Press,* June 28, 1982 at 3A, cited in Note, *What's Wrong with Fetal Rights,* 10 Harv. Women's L.J. 9, 47 (1987).

223. *Fleeing the Law,* at 4A.

224. *Id.* at 3A.

225. Unpublished opinion, No. 84-7-50006-0 at 4 (Super. Ct. of Benton County, April 20, 1984), discussed at 10 Harv. Women's L.J. at 51 N. 215 (1987).

226. *Id.*

227. 42 N.J. 421, 201 A.2d 537 (per curiam), cert. denied 377 U.S. 985 (1964).

228. 42 N.J. at 423, 201 A.2d at 538.

229. *Id.* The court acknowledged that this issue was more complex than the issue of a fetus' right to receive medical treatment.

230. 67 N.J. Super 517, 171 A.2d 140 (1961).

231. 171 A.2d at 141.

232. *Id.* at 143 (emphasis added).

233. *Id.*

234. 388 Mass. 331, 446 N.E.2d 395 (1983).

235. *Id.* at 332, 446 N.E.2d at 396.

236. *Id.*

237. *Id.* at 334, 446 N.E.2d at 397.

238. *Id.*

239. *Id.*

240. See *Note—Legal Rights,* supra, Note 209, at 727. See also B. Keplinger and J. Cramer, *Wrongful Pregnancy: A House Divided,* 23 Tort & Insur. L.J. 496, 498 (1988) ("the majority of jurisdictions which have considered the question have recognized a cause of action for wrongful pregnancy").

241. 648 S.W.2d 861 (Ky. 1983).

242. *Id.* at 862.

243. *Id.*

244. *Id.* at 862.

245. *James G. v. Caserta,* 332 S.E.2d 872, 877 n.7 (W. Va. 1985).

246. See *Note—Legal Rights,* supra, Note 209, at 735.

247. See also *Public Health Trust v. Brown,* 388 So.2d 1084 (Fla. Dist. Ct. App. 1988).

248. *Flowers v. District of Columbia,* 478 A.2d 1073, 1076 (D.C. 1982).

249. See *Note—Legal Rights,* supra, Note 209, at 73.

250. *Id.*

251. *Id.* (emphasis supplied) (citation omitted).

252. 299 Md. 257, 473 A.2d 429 (1984).

253. *Id.* at 430.

254. *Id.*

255. *Id.* at 431.

256. *Id.*

257. *Id.*

258. *Id.* at 435.

259. *Id.* at 436–37.

260. *Id.* at 438.

261. 251 Cal. App. 2d 303, 59 Cal. Rptr. 463 (Cal. Ct. App. 1967).

262. 59 Cal. Rptr. at 476.

263. *Id.* at 477 (emphasis added).

264. 48 Ohio St.2d 41, 356 N.E.2d 496 (1976).

265. 356 N.E.2d at 498.

266. *Id.*

267. *Id.* at 498 n.1.

268. 361 So.2d 546 (Ala. 1978).

269. *Id.* at 548 (emphasis added).

270. 69 Wis.2d 766, 233 N.W.2d 372 (1975).

271. 233 N.W.2d at 373.

272. *Id.* at 374.

273. *Id.*

274. *Id.* at 375–76 (emphasis added) (citation omitted).

275. 97 N.J. 339, 478 A.2d 755 (1984).

276. 478 A.2d at 758.

277. *Id.*

278. *Id.* at 762.

279. *Id.* at 762. See also *Siemieniec v. Lutheran General Hospital,* 134 Ill. App. 3d 823, 480 N.E.2d 1227 (1985).

280. 138 Mass. 14 (1884).

281. *Id.* at 22.

282. W. Prosser, *Handbook of the Law of Torts,* Section 55, at 336 (4th ed. 1971).

283. 65 F. Supp. 138 (D.D.C. 1946).

284. *Id.* at 143.

285. *Id.* at 142.

286. Viability is defined as "[t]hat stage of fetal development when the life of the unborn child may be continued indefinitely outside the womb by natural or artificial life support systems." *Black's Law Dictionary* 1404 (5th ed. 1979).

287. 282 A.D.2d 542, 125 N.Y.S.2d 696 (1953).

288. 125 N.Y.S.2d at 698.

289. 67 Ill. 2d 348, 367 N.E.2d 1250 (1977).

290. 367 N.E.2d at 1255.

291. 78 A.D.2d 389, 434 N.Y.S.2d 401 (1981).

292. 434 N.Y.S.2d at 401.

293. Plaintiff's birth on June 3, 1976 suggests his conception occurred around September 1975. 434 N.Y.S.2d at 401.

294. 434 N.Y.S.2d at 401.

295. *Id.* at 403.

Chapter III

1. This award was later reduced on appeal to $5.5 million. See *Christian v. Sheft,* No. 574 153 (Super. Ct. L.A. Co.).

2. See *Herpes Virus Infection,* Scientific American, Inc. (1988). See Note, *Liability in Tort for the Sexual Transmission of Disease — Genital Herpes and the Law,* 70 Corn. L.Rev. 101, 108 (1984).

3. See *Jury Makes Award to Woman After Death of Ex-Husband,* AIDS Policy & Law (BNA) at 5 (Jan. 25, 1989).

4. See *Prosser and Keeting on the Law of Torts,* W. Page Keeting, editor at pp. 164–165 (5th ed. 1984) (hereinafter *Prosser and Keeting*).

5. 175 Ga. App. 538, 333 S.E.2d 852 (1985).

6. 33 S.E.2d at 854.

7. *Id.* at 855.

8. *Id.* (citation omitted).

9. *Id.* at 856.

10. 312 Md. 135, 538 A.2d 1175 (Md. 1988).

11. 538 A.2d at 1177.

12. *Id.*

13. *Id.* at 1178.

14. *Id.* at 1179.

15. *Id.*

16. *Berner v. Caldwell,* 87-646, cited in *The National Law Journal,* May 1, 1989, p. 6.

17. See *Prosser and Keeting,* supra Note 4, at p. 728. See also *B.N. v. K.K.,* 312 Md. 135, 538 A.2d 1175, 1182 (Md. 1988).

18. 150 Cal. App.3d 992, 198 Cal. Rptr. 273 (1984).

19. 150 Cal. App.3d at 994.

20. *Id.*

21. *Id.*

22. *Id.* at 996.

23. *Id.* at 996–97.

24. 538 A.2d at 1182.

25. *Id.* at 1183.

26. *Id.*

27. *Id* at 1184.

28. *Id.*

29. *Id.*

30. W. Prosser, (4th ed.) at 697.

31. R. Prentice and P. Murray, *Liability for Transmission of Herpes: Using Traditional Principles to Encourage Honesty in Sexual Relationships,* 11 Journal of Contemporary Law 67, 77 (hereinafter *Honesty*).

32. 123 A.D.2d 165, 510 N.Y.S.2d 104 (1986).

33. 310 N.Y.S.2d at 105.

34. *Id.*

35. *Id.* at 107.

36. See *Restatement (Second) of Torts*, Section 21 (1965). See also *Prosser and Keeting,* supra, Note 4, at p. 43.

37. See *Prosser and Keeting,* at p. 39.

38. 102 A. 63 (Del. Ct. Gen. Sess. 1917).

39. *Id.* at 64 (emphasis added).

40. See *Prosser and Keeting,* supra, Note 4, at pp. 54 et seq. See also *Restatement (Second) of Torts*, Section 46(1) (1965).

41. Leo, "The New Scarlet Letter," *Time,* Aug. 2, 1982 at 64.

42. 538 A.2d at 1180.

43. *Id.*

44. *Id.* at 1181.

45. *Id.* at 1182.

46. See *Honesty*, supra, Note 31, p. 80–81.

47. *Prosser and Keeting,* at p. 112.

48. *Id.*

49. 6 Idaho 317, 55 P. at 656 (1989).

50. 55 P. at 657.

51. *Id.*

52. *Id.* at 658.

53. *Restatement (Second) of Torts,* Section 892b (1979).

54. 176 Eng. Rep. 925.

55. *Id.*

56. See *Prosser and Keeting,* supra, Note 4, at p. 486–87.

57. *Id.* at p. 451–52.

58. *Id.* at p. 471 et seq.

59. Milwaukee, Wis. County Circuit Court, No. 707-357, Jan. 15, 1988, reported in 31 ATLA L. Rep. 273 (Aug. 1988).

60. Reported in the *Wall Street Journal,* Jan. 18, 1990, p. B-8.

61. 1 *W. Blackstone Commentaries,* 430.

62. *Restatement (Second) of Torts,* 895(f)(i) (1979).

63. 180 N.C. 516, 105 S.E. 206 (1920).

64. 105 S.E. at 207.

65. *Id.* at 209–210.

66. 29 Del. 594, 102 A. 63 (Del. Ct. Gen. Sess. 1917).

67. 241 So. 2d 752 (Fla. Dist. Ct. App. 1970).
68. *Id.* at 753.
69. *Id.*
70. *Id.*
71. 131 Cal. Rptr. 14, 551 P.2d 334 (Cal. 1976).
72. 131 Cal. Rptr. at 19.
73. *Id.* at 20.
74. *Id.* at 27 (emphasis added).
75. *Id.*
76. 177 N.W. 831 (Neb. 1920).
77. *Id.* at 831.
78. *Id.* at 832.
79. *Id.* (emphasis added).
80. Rinaldi, HIV Blood Test Counseling: AMA Physicians Guidelines (AMA 1988).
81. Closen and Isaacman, *Notifying Private Third Parties at Risk for HIV Infection, TRIAL* 50, 52 (May 1989).
82. *Id.*
83. See *The National Law Journal,* p. 6, April 17, 1989.

Chapter IV

1. 42 U.S.C. Section 2000(e)-2(a) (1).
2. 42 U.S.C. Section 2000(e)-(2)(a) (1976).
3. 42 U.S.C. Section 2000(e)-2(a) (2).
4. 42 U.S.C. Section 2000(e)(b).
5. 42 U.S.C. Section 2000(e)-16(a).
6. *International Brotherhood of Teamsters v. U.S.,* 431 U.S. 324, 335 n.15 (1977).
7. *Id.* at note 44.
8. 647 F.2d 441 (4th Cir. 1981).
9. *Id.* at 443.
10. *Id.*
11. *Id.*
12. *Id.*
13. *Id.*
14. *Id.* at 443–44.
15. *Id.* at 444, citing 42 U.S.C. Section 2000(e)-2(a) (2).
16. *Id.*
17. *Id.* at 445.
18. *Id.* at 446.
19. 536 F. Supp. 435 (W.D. Wisc. 1982).
20. *Id.* at 437.
21. *Id.* at 438.
22. *Id.*
23. *Id.*
24. *Id.* at 440.
25. *Id.* at 442.
26. *Id.* at 443.

27. *Id.* at 448–49.
28. *Id.*
29. See *McDonnell Douglas Corp. v. Green,* 411 U.S. 792, 802 (1973).
30. 401 U.S. 424 (1971).
31. *Id.* at 426.
32. *Id.* at 429–30.
33. *Id.* at 430.
34. *Id.* at 431.
35. *Id.*
36. *Id.* at 433.
37. *Id.* at 432–33.
38. 109 S. Ct. 2115 (1989).
39. 619 F.2d 611, *cert. denied* 449 U.S. 872 (1980).
40. *Id.* at 613–14.
41. *Id.* at 614.
42. *Id.*
43. *Id.* at 616.
44. *Id.* at 685.
45. *Id.* at 615.
46. 438 U.S. 567 (1978).
47. *Id.* at 577.
48. *Id.* at 577–78 (citation omitted).
49. *Id.* at 578.
50. *Texas Dept. of Community Affairs v. Burdine,* 450 U.S. 248, 260 (1981).
51. 697 F.2d 1172 (4th Cir. 1982).
52. *Id.* at 1176.
53. *Id.* at 1188.
54. *Id.*
55. *Id.*
56. 886 F. 2d 871, *cert. granted* (89–1215).
57. 42 U.S.C. 2000(e)-2(e)(1).
58. 433 U.S. 321 (1977).
59. *Id.* at 328–29.
60. *Id.* at 331.
61. *Id.*
62. *Id.* at 332.
63. *Id.* at 334.
64. *Id.* at 335.
65. *Id.* at 335–36.
66. *Id.* at 336–37.
67. 442 F.2d 385 (5th Cir. 1971).
68. *Id.* at 388.
69. *Id.*
70. *Id.*
71. *Id.*
72. *Id.* at 388–89 (emphasis added).
73. 450 U.S. 248 (1981).
74. *Id.* at 2–4.

75. 422 U.S. 405 (1975).

76. *Id.* at 410–11.

77. *Id.* at 431.

78. 408 F.2d 228 (5th Cir. 1969).

79. *Id.* at 234.

80. *Id.*

81. *Id.* at 235.

82. *Id.* at 236 (emphasis added).

83. 29 CFR Section 1604.1(III).

84. U.S. Constitution, Fourteenth Amendment.

85. 578 F. Supp. 1209 (D.N.J. 1984).

86. *Id.* at 1216.

87. See, e.g., *Strong v. Demopolis City Board of Education,* 515 F. Supp. 730 (D. Ala. 1981).

88. U.S. Constitution, Fifth Amendment.

89. 519 F. Supp. 517 (N.D. Ill. 1981).

90. *Id.* at 518–19.

91. *Id.* at 521.

92. *Id.* at 522.

93. 29 U.S.C. 206(d)(1).

94. 29 U.S.C. 206 (e)(1).

95. 590 F.2d 128 (5th Cir. 1979).

96. *Id.* at 130.

97. *Id.*

98. *Id.* at 133.

99. See, e.g. Ariz. Rev. Stat. Ann. Section 23-341 (1983); N.Y. Labor Code Section 194 (1986).

100. The Pregnancy Discrimination Act, Pub.L. No. 95-555, amending U.S.C. Section 2000(e)-*et seq.* (Supp. 111 1979).

101. 44 F.R. 23805, Ap. 20, 1979. The remainder of the EEOC's guidelines provide:

> (b) Disabilities caused or contributed to by pregnancy, childbirth or related medical conditions, for all job-related purposes, shall be treated the same as disabilities caused or contributed to by other medical conditions, under any health or disability insurance or sick leave plan available in connection with employment. Written or unwritten employment policies and practices involving matters such as the commencement and duration of leave, the availability of extensions, the accrual of seniority and other benefits and privileges, reinstatement, and payment under any health or disability insurance or sick leave plan, formal or informal, shall be applied to disability due to pregnancy, childbirth or related medical conditions on the same terms and conditions as they are applied to other disabilities. Health insurance benefits for abortion, except where the life of the mother would be endangered if the fetus were carried to term or where medical complications have arisen from an abortion, are not required to be paid by an employer; nothing herein, however, precludes an employer from providing abortion benefits or otherwise affects bargaining agreements in regard to abortion.

(c) Where the termination of an employee who is temporarily disabled is caused by an employment policy under which insufficient or no leave is available, such a termination violates the Act if it has a disparate impact on employees of one sex and is not justified by business necessity.

(d)(1) Any fringe benefit program or fund, or insurance program which is in effect on October 31, 1978, which does not treat women affected by pregnancy, childbirth, or related medical conditions the same as other persons not so affected but similar in their ability or inability to work, must be in compliance with the provisions of Section 1604.10(b) by April 29, 1979. In order to come into compliance with provisions of 1604.10(b), there can be no reduction of benefits or compensation which were in effect on October 31, 1978, before October 31, 1979 or the expiration of a collective bargaining agreement in effect on October 31, 1978, whichever is later.

(2) Any fringe benefit program implemented after October 31, 1978, must comply with the provisions of Section 1604.10(b) upon implementation.

102. See 29 C.F.R. pt. 1604.
103. 414 U.S. 632 (1974).
104. *Id.* at 634.
105. *Id.* at 640–41.
106. *Id.* at 644.
107. 730 F.2d 994 (5th Cir. 1984).
108. *Id.* at 999.
109. See 29 C.F.R. Section 1604.10(c) (1980).
110. See Cal. Govt. Code Ann. Section 12945.
111. 29 C.F.R. Section 1604.11(a). The remainder of the EEOC's guidelines provides:

(b) *In determining whether alleged conduct constitutes sexual harassment,* the Commission will look at the record as a whole and at the totality of the circumstances, such as the nature of the sexual advances and the context in which the alleged incidents occurred. The determination of the legality of a particular action will be made from the facts, on a case by case basis.

(c) Applying general Title VII principles, an *employer,* employment agency, joint apprenticeship committee or labor organization (hereinafter collectively referred to as "employer") *is responsible for its acts and those of its agents and supervisory employees with respect to sexual harassment* regardless of whether the specific acts complained of were authorized or even forbidden by the employer and regardless of whether the employer knew or should have known of their occurrence. The Commission will examine the circumstances of the particular employment relationship and the job functions performed by the individual in determining whether an individual acts in either a supervisory or agency capacity.

(d) *With respect to conduct between fellow employees,* an employer is responsible for acts of sexual harassment in the workplace where the employer (or its agents or supervisory employees) knows or should have known of the conduct, unless it can show that it took immediate and appropriate corrective action.

(e) *An employer may also be responsible for the acts of nonemployees,* with respect to sexual harassment of employees in the workplace, where the employer (or its agents or supervisory employees) knows or should have known of the conduct and fails to take immediate and appropriate corrective action. In reviewing these cases the Commission will consider the extent of the employer's control and any other legal responsibility which the employer may have with respect to the conduct of such nonemployees.

(f) Prevention is the best tool for the elimination of sexual harassment. An employer should take all steps necessary to prevent sexual harassment from occurring, such as affirmatively raising the subject, expressing strong disapproval, developing appropriate sanctions, informing employees of their right to raise and how to raise the issue of harassment under Title VII, and developing methods to sensitize all concerned.

(g) Other related practices: Where employment opportunities or benefits are granted because of an individual's submission to the employer's sexual advances or requests for sexual favors, the employer may be held liable for unlawful sex discrimination against other persons who were qualified for but denied that employment opportunity or benefit. *See also* Title VII, Pub.L. 88-352, 78 Stat. 253 (42 U.S.C. Sections 2000e et seq.).

112. 477 U.S. 57 (1986).

113. *Id.* at 60.

114. *Id.*

115. *Id.* at 67–68.

116. *Id.* at 62.

117. *Id.* at 68 (emphasis supplied).

118. *Id.* at 69 (quoting 29 C.F.R. Section 1604.11(b) [1985]).

119. See, e.g. *Williams v. Saxbe,* 413 F. Supp. 654, 657 (D.D.C. 1976), *rev'd on other grounds sub nom Williams v. Bell,* 587 F.2d 1240 (D.C. Cir. 1978) (female employee whose resistance to male supervisor's sexual advances results in job related retaliatory action has cause of action under Title VII).

120. 29 C.F.R. Section 1604.11(a).

121. 477 U.S. 57, 67 (quoting *Henson v. Dundee,* 682 F.2d 897, 904 [11th Cir. 1982]).

122. 477 U.S. at 68–69. The EEOC Guidelines provide that sexual harassment claims be considered in light of the totality of the circumstances. See, e.g., 29 C.F.R. Section 1604.11(b).

123. *Id.* at 67, quoting *Henson v. Dundee,* 682 F.2d 897, 904 (11th Cir. 1982).

124. *Id.* at 71–72 (quoting EEOC Amicus Curiae Brief at 22).

125. See, Note, *Meritor Savings Bank v. Vinson: Sexual Harassment at Work,* 10 Harv. W.L.J. 203, 218 N.91 (1987).

126. See Fair Empl. Prac. Man. 401: 6094–98 (citing *Restatement (Second) of Agency [1985]).*

127. 413 F. Supp. 654 (D.D.C. 1976).
128. *Id.* at 655.
129. *Id.* at 655–56.
130. *Id.* at 657.
131. *Id.*
132. *Id.* at 662 (emphasis added).
133. *Bundy v. Jackson,* 641 F.2d 934, 1161 (D.D.C. Cir. 1981).
134. *Id.*
135. *Id.* at 938.
136. *Id.* at 944.
137. *Id.* at 940.
138. *Id.*
139. *Id.* at 943.
140. *Id.* at 945 (emphasis added).
141. *Id.*
142. *Id.* at 948 (emphasis added).
143. 793 F.2d 714 (5th Cir. 1986).
144. *Id.* at 716.
145. *Id.* at 722.
146. *Id.* at 720.
147. *Id.* at 721 n.7.
148. 589 F. Supp. 780 (E.D. Wisc. 1984).
149. *Id.* at 782–83.
150. *Id.* at 783.
151. *Id.* at 784.
152. *Id.*
153. 605 F. Supp. 1047 (N.D. Ill. 1985), *aff'd* 798 F.2d 210 (7th Cir. 1986).
154. *Id.* at 1050–51.
155. *Id.* at 1051.
156. *Id.* at 1055 (emphasis added).

Chapter V

1. These laws are the subject of Chapter 4.
2. 793 F.2d 113 (5th Cir. 1986).
3. *Id.* at 114.
4. See *Aiello v. United Airlines, Inc.,* 818 F.2d 1196 (5th Cir. 1987).
5. *See, e.g.,* Civil Rights Acts Amendments of 1981: Hearings on HR 1454 before the Subcommittee on Employment Opportunities of the House Committee on Education and Labor, 97th Cong., 2nd Sess. 1–2 (1982).
6. 608 F.2d 327 (9th Cir. 1979).
7. *Id.* at 329.
8. *Id.* 329–30.
9. *Id.* at 330–31.
10. Wis. Stat. Ann. Sections 111.321–.395 (West 1988).
11. *Id.* at 111.36(d)(1).
12. See *Developments in the Law — Sexual Orientation and the Law,*

102 Harv. L. Rev. 1058, 1668, n51 (1989). *See, e.g.*, D.C. Code Ann. Section 1-2502 (1981 and Supp. 1985).

13. 32 C.F.R. Part 41, App. A, Pt. 1.H., et seq. (1989).
14. See *Id.* Pt. 1.H.I.C.
15. See *Id.* Pt. 1.E.4.
16. 735 F.2d 1220 (10th Cir. 1984).
17. *Id.* at 1222.
18. *Id.* at 1224.
19. *Id.*
20. *Id.* at 1226–27.
21. *Id.* at 1227.
22. *Id.* at 1227–28 n.7.
23. *Id.* at 1228.
24. *Id.* at 1229.
25. *Id.*
26. See, e.g., *Benshalom v. Marsh,* 703 F. Supp. 1372 (E.D. Wis. 1989).
27. *Id.*
28. *Id.*
29. See 32 C.F.R. Part 41, App. A Pt. 1.H.2.
30. See 32 C.F.R. Part 41, App. A, Pt. 1.H.i. c(1) (1989).
31. See *Id.* Pt. 1.H.1. c(2).
32. See *Id.* Pt. 1.H.1. c(3).
33. See, e.g., *Padula v. Webster,* 822 F.2d 97 (D.C. Cir. 1987) (discussing FBI ban on employing gay males or lesbians); *Dubbs v. C.I.A.,* 866 F.2d 1114 (9th Cir. 1989) (discussing C.I.A. refusal to issue security clearance to gay males or lesbians).
34. 417 F.2d 1161 (D.C. Cir. 1969).
35. *Id.* at 1162–63.
36. *Id.* at 1165 (emphasis added).
37. See 5 C.F.R. Section 731.202(b)(2) (1988).
38. See, e.g., *Woodward v. U.S.,* 86-1283 (Fed. Cir. March 29, 1989) Lexis, Gen. Fed. Library, Court's file. See also, *Padula v. Webster,* 822 F.2d 97 (D.C. Cir. 1987).
39. See, e.g., Ala. Code Section 13A-6-65(a)(3) (1982); Ga. Code Ann. Section 16-6-2 (1988); Idaho Code Section 18-6605 (1987).
40. 106 S. Ct. 2841, 478 U.S. 186 (1986).
41. The Georgia statute provided that "a person commits the offense of sodomy when he performs or submits to any sexual act involving sex organs of one person and the mouth or anus of another." Ga. Code Ann. Section 16-6-2 1988, cited at 106 S. Ct. at 2842 n.1.
42. 106 S. Ct. at 2843 (citations omitted).
43. *Id.* at 2844.
44. *Id.* at 2844–55.
45. *Id.* at 2846.
46. *Id.*
47. *Id.*
48. *Id.* at 2843.
49. For example, the constitutionality of the Massachusetts sodomy law, as applied to private consensual conduct, remains uncertain after the decision

of the Massachusetts Supreme Court in *Commonwealth v. Balthazar,* 366 Mass. 298, 302, 318 N.E.2d 478, 481 (1974). See also *Kentucky v. Wasson,* No. 86 M859 slip op. at 2 (Fayette Dist. Ct. October 31, 1986). In this case, a Kentucky court held that a state sodomy statute violated the right to privacy protected by the Kentucky Constitution.

50. 388 U.S. 1 (1967).

51. *Id.* at 12 (quoting *Skinner v. Oklahoma,* 316 U.S. 535, 541 [1942]).

52. 486 F. Supp. 1119 (C.D. Cal. 1980), *aff'd* 673 F.2d 1036 (95h Cir. 1982), *cert. denied,* 458 U.S. 1111 (1982).

53. *Id.* at 1120-21.

54. *Id.* at 1124.

55. *Id.* at 1124-25.

56. 11 Wash. App. 247, 522 P.2d 1187 (1974).

57. 522 P.2d at 1188-89, 1190.

58. *Id.* at 1194-95.

59. 106 Misc.2d 792, 435 N.Y.S.2d 527 (1981).

60. 63 N.Y.2d 233, 471 N.E.2d 424 (1984).

61. 471 N.E.2d at 425.

62. *See, e.g.,* Colo. Rev. Stat. Section 14-10-124 (1987); Me. Rev. Stat. Ann. tit. 19, Section 752 (Supp. 1988); N.Y. Dom. Rel. Law Section 240 (McKinney Supp. 1989); Pa. Stat. Ann. tit. 23, Sections 5301, 5303 (Purdon Supp. 1988).

63. 745 S.W.2d 726, (Mo. Ct. App. 1987).

64. *Id.* at 727.

65. *Id.*

66. *Id.* at 728.

67. See, e.g., *In re Marriage of Birdsall,* 197 Ca. App. 3d 1924, 243 Cal. Rptr. 287 (1988); *Guinan v. Guinan,* 102 A.D.2d 963, 477 N.Y.S.2d 830 (1984).

68. See, e.g., *S.N.E. v. R.L.B.,* 699 P.2d 875 (Alaska 1985); *D.H. v. J.H.,* 418 N.E.2d 286 (Ind. Ct. App. 1981); *Doe v. Doe,* 16 Mass. App. Ct. 499, 452 N.E.2d 293 (1983); *In re J.S. & C.,* 129 N.J. Super. 486, 324 A.2d 90 (Ch. Div. 1974), *aff'd* 142 N.J. Super. 499, 362 A.2d 254 (1976); *Stroman v. Williams,* 291 S.C. 376, 353 S.E.2d 704 (Ct. App. 1987); *Rowsey v. Rowsey,* 329 S.E.2d 57 (W. Va. 1985).

69. See, e.g., *DiStefano v. DiStefano,* 60 A.D.2d 976, 401 N.Y.S.2d 636 (1978).

70. See, e.g., *J.L.P.(H.) v. D.J.P.,* 643 S.W.2d 865 (Mo. Ct. App. 1982).

71. See Freed & Walker, *Family Law in the Fifty States: An Overview,* 21 Fam. L.Q. 417, 441-42 (1988) (reporting that 20 states retain traditional "fault" grounds for divorce in addition to one or more "no-fault" grounds).

72. N.Y. Dom. Rel. Law Section 170(4) (McKinney 1988).

73. See, e.g., *M.V.R. v. T.M.R.,* 115 Misc.2d 674, 454 N.Y.S.2d 779, 783 N.11 (1982).

Chapter VI

1. See, e.g., Centers for Disease Control, *Update: Acquired Immunodeficiency Syndrome — United States.* 35 Morbidity & Mortality Weekly Rep. 757-66 (1986).

2. 29 U.S.C. Section 701 et seq. (1982 & Supp. IV 1986).

3. See 29 U.S.C. Section 794.

4. 107 S. Ct. 1123 (1987).

5. *Id.* at 1128.

6. *Id.* at 1130–31.

7. *Id.* at 1131 (citation omitted).

8. *Id.* at 1128 N.7.

9. 45 Empl. Prac. Dec. par. 37,782 P. 51,025 (CCH) (9th Cir. 1988).

10. *Id.* at par. 1151,029, citing U.S. Public Health Service, Surgeon General's Report on Acquired Immunodeficiency Syndrome at 13 (1986).

11. *Id.* at par. 51,030.

12. *Id.*

13. *Id.* at par. 51,033.

14. The report of the National Gay Rights Activists may be found at Daily Lab. Rep. (BNA) No. 182 at A-16 (Sept. 19, 1986).

15. Tennessee later amended its handicapped discrimination statute to specifically exclude contagious diseases from the definition of handicapped. See *Tenn. Code Ann.* Section 8-50-103(c) (Supp. 1987).

16. FCHR No. 85-0624 (Dec. 11, 1985) (*reprinted in* Daily Lab. Rep. (BNA) No. 242 at E-1-E-6 (Dec. 17, 1985), *aff'd* April 7, 1986, reported in 1 AIDS Policy and Law (BNA) No. 7, at 1 (April 23, 1986).

17. Fla. St. Ann. Section 760.01 (West 1986).

18. *Shuttleworth,* Daily Lab. Rep. (BNA) No. 242 at E-1-E-6, E1 (Dec. 17, 1985); 649 F. Supp. 35 (S.D. Fla. 1986).

19. Daily Lab. Rep. (BNA) No. 237, at A-8 (Dec. 10, 1986).

20. Cal. Fair Employ. and Housing Commission Dec. No. 87-12 (1987) *aff'd* 46 F.E.P. 1089 (Cal. Super. Ct. 1988).

21. Case No. EH-35287 (Sept. 1, 1988) *reported in* Daily Lab. Rep. (BNA) No. 197, at A-2–A-3 (Oct. 12, 1988).

22. See, e.g., Beldon & Donelan, *Discrimination Against People with AIDS: The Public Perception,* 319 New Eng. J. Med. 1022 (1988) (discussing a 1987 Gallup Poll Survey).

23. *Shuttleworth,* Daily Lab. Rep. (BNA) No. 242 at E-1-E-6, E1 (Dec. 17, 1985); 649 F. Supp. 35 (S.D. Fla. 1986).

24. Daily Lab. Rep. (BNA) No. 242 at E-2, E-4.

25. *Id.* at E-2.

26. 46 Fair Empl. Prac. Cas. (BNA) 279, 287 (9th Cir. 1988).

27. 540 F. Supp. 910 (E.D. Pa. 1982).

28. 497 F. Supp. 1088 (D. Hawaii 1980).

29. See, e.g., Section 510.

30. See *Folz v. Marriott Corp.,* 594 F. Supp. 1007 (W.D. Mo. 1984).

31. Cal. Health and Safety Code Section 199.20–199.22 (1985).

32. Fla. Stat. Ann. Section 381.606(4)(a), (5) (West Supp. 1987).

33. Mass. Ann. Laws Ch. 111 Section 70F (Law Co-Op Supp. 1987).

34. Wis. Stat. Ann. Section 103.15 et seq. (West Supp. 1987).

35. See, e.g., *Local 1812 American Fed'n of Gov't Employees v. U.S. Dept. of State,* 662 F. Supp. 50 (D.D.C. 1987). Compare *Glover v. Eastern Neb. Comm. Office of Retardation,* 686 F. Supp. 243 (D. Neb. 1988).

36. See, e.g., Cal. Civ. Code Section 56.05 et seq. (West 1985).

37. See, e.g., *Woods v. White,* 681 F. Supp. 874 (W.D. Wis. 1988).

38. See *NY Times,* Feb. 14, 1986, at A-12, col. 2.

39. *Brown v. Board of Education,* 347 U.S. 483, 493 (1954).

40. E. Cooper, *AIDS Law: The Impact of AIDS on American Schools and Prisons,* 1987 Annual Survey of American Law 117, 122 (1987).

41. 130 Misc.2d 398, 502 N.Y.S.2d 325 (Sup. Ct. 1986).

Index